D1737022

Papa Rossi's Secrets Of
Italian Cooking

PAPA ROSSI'S SECRETS OF

Italian Cooking

Victor Bennett
with
Antonia Rossi

GRAMERCY PUBLISHING COMPANY • NEW YORK

Dedicated to
Mama Marcellette Rossi,
without whose encouragement and help
this volume would
never have been written

Dominic "Papa" Rossi, now deceased, had his own Italian restaurant in San Francisco for over forty years. He was widely known on the West Coast as one of the patriarchs of fine Italian cuisine in this country. This book has been prepared as a loving tribute to his memory by his daughter, Antonia Rossi and foster son, Victor Bennett.

INTRODUCTION

Papa Dominic Rossi was born in 1885 in the province of Martina in southern Italy. In those days, the professions or trades to be followed by the sons in the family were determined by the father long before the boys reached the age of twenty-one. Papa Rossi's family was no exception to this tradition. One brother promised to study medicine, one law and Papa to become a priest. He entered the seminary when very young, and there he became skillful in making rare and appealing liqueurs and wines. Two weeks before becoming ordained, Papa Rossi divulged the long-harbored secret that the priesthood was not for him. He told his uncles of his desire to see the world and his wish to visit America. He could not, he told them, commit his life to serving mankind through the church, and the promise made to his father years before must be broken. With the assurances of his uncles that he was no longer held by his promise, and with the money received from the sale of his share of the family land, he left for Naples to find a ship bound for the United States. In 1906 he arrived in Utica, New York, with one suitcase, a zabaglione pan and $2,600.

Papa began his new life by purchasing new clothes and making new friends. Several months later, down to his last $5.00, he went to work in a small restaurant for $6.00 a week. In his second week there, his salary was raised to $12.00.

In 1909 Papa Rossi married, and when his daughter Antonia was born several years later, his happiness was complete. Six months later, tragedy struck: Mrs. Rossi became seriously ill and passed away. Antonia was placed with relatives and Papa joined the United States Navy, serving until the end of World War I.

After the war, Papa settled in southern California and became Head Property Man for Western Costume and Manufacturing Company in Hollywood. Among some of his closest friends were Edgar Rice Burroughs and Douglas Fairbanks, Sr. Besides making swords, which would swash and buckle on command, for Mr. Fairbanks, Papa spent his leisure hours creating delectable liqueurs and wines which he presented to his friends and associates.

I met Papa Rossi for the first time when I was seven years old, shortly after he had met my mother, Marcellette. Little did I realize then that their meeting and marriage would have such an overwhelming effect on my life. As I watched the sheer joy they derived from preparing food and drink for guests, a desire to create foods was awakened in me, and by the ripe old age of ten, with Papa's guidance, food and its preparation had become the most important part of my life.

Weekend after weekend I saw Italian feasts prepared by Mama and Papa Rossi for twenty or thirty guests, and homemade wine or liqueurs were always served. (I believe the only reason they were never "caught" for making the then-prohibited alcoholic beverages was that they never sold them, but used them only for serving in their own home or as gifts to their friends.) On numerous occasions their friends offered to pool their resources and back them in a restaurant, and Papa himself had always said, "One of these days Marcy and I will open our own restaurant."

In 1930 Mama and Papa gave up their positions and took me out of military school, and we moved to San Francisco. Papa went to work as chef at the old Lucca Restaurant, where you could eat all you wanted for fifty cents.

After four years in San Francisco, a dream came true. Mama and Papa Rossi opened their own restaurant, The Royal Kitchen, located at 1623 California Street, San Francisco. It was an immediate success. After one year, they were able to buy their own home for the then-staggering price of $6,500.

The Royal Kitchen became my training ground for every phase of the restaurant business. Papa Rossi started me as dishwasher after school, and just before I got dishpan hands, he made me assistant cook, then lunch cook, sauce cook and finally out front as waiter.

For fourteen years The Royal Kitchen, under Mama's and Papa's guidance, flourished. During those years their home was again filled with guests enjoying fine Italian food and wines. But Papa's secret desire had always been to live in the country in a small settlement like Martina, a place where he could have his own land and grow vegetables and fruits. Such a place was in Paradise, California, situated northeast of Oroville, not too far from the Feather River. Papa decided instantly that he and Mama had to live in this little village with its small, intimate, privately-owned shops scattered through the hills among pine and fir trees. In less than a week, the seven acres of paradise were purchased, The Royal Kitchen was sold along with the home in San Francisco and their entire attention was focused on building a home in this newfound village. Papa became a carpenter and, with his hands and no help other than Mama's, built his ideal country home. When the house was completed, Papa turned to planting his fruit trees and garden. As vegetables and fruits grew and matured, he cooked and served foods such as he had eaten as a little boy in Italy, only this time the food was for his family and friends. The love of family was never more predominate in any father than it was in Papa Rossi when his daughter Antonia would fly out from New York to visit. Then the kitchen was bedlam with Mama and Papa scurrying around, arguing a little at times, and each trying to outdo the other. But all survived to enjoy the delicacies from the kitchen prepared with thought and loving care.

I became a part of that happy home when I could arrange to take time off from my duties as headwaiter on Matson's luxury liner, the *Lurline*. Each time Papa and I were together, the topic of our conversation was food. Each time Mama or Papa would ask me what I wanted to eat, I would reply, "beans." Out of this grew the idea for my *Complete Bean Cookbook*, published by Prentice-Hall in 1967.

Whenever Papa saw me working on my cookbook he had many fine suggestions and ideas. One day I asked him why he didn't write an Italian cookbook—and so it began. But before its completion, Papa died at the age of eighty-three. In attempting to complete Papa's book, I discovered that I was too close to it, so I called Antonia for assistance. Hopefully you will agree when I say that she has completed an authentic, informative cookbook. You have it in your hands. You be the judge.

Papa Rossi will be guiding you in these recipes just as he and Mama guided me with the encouragement and understanding that wonderful parents can give a son. They taught me faith and pride in creating from the raw materials the Lord bestowed on us "a feast fit for a king," on any income, any budget, at any time, regardless of surroundings. *Buòn appetito!*

Victor Bennett

CONTENTS

Papa Rossi's Secrets of
Italian Cooking

Antipasto

Antipasto literally means "before the pasta" (the spaghetti or macaroni course). It is an appetizer, a few bites of flavorful food to make the mouth water and whet the appetite for the meal to follow.

A stimulating beginning to an Italian dinner is a platter brimming with antipasto. Make your selection from the large variety of foods so readily accessible in today's markets: thinly sliced meats such as salami, prosciutto (the Italian ham), peppery sausages; cheeses like Gorgonzola, provolone, Romano, for a sharp, piquant taste; marinated mushrooms, anchovies, marinated fish, peppers, green onions, hard-boiled eggs, olives, crisp raw vegetables in season. Cold boiled meats, marinated in different salse, make an excellent antipasto. Or try ceci marinara, pickled beans of all varieties or pizza cut into bite-size pieces. An antipasto salad is also very savory.

This is a wonderful opportunity to use your creativeness and assemble an antipasto platter which is colorful and mouth-watering. But remember to keep the servings small, as your purpose is to stimulate, not satiate, the appetite.

ANTIPASTO SALAD

READY TRAY   Serves 4 to 6

 6   tablespoons olive oil
 2   cloves garlic, gently crushed
 3   tablespoons wine vinegar
 1   teaspoon fresh basil, finely chopped
 ½   pound fresh white mushroom caps, thinly sliced
 ¼   pound sliced boiled ham, julienned
 2   ounces white truffles, thinly sliced
 ½   cup finely chopped celery hearts
     Salt and freshly ground black pepper

> Heat 2 tablespoons oil in small skillet over low flame. Add garlic and sauté until brown, then discard garlic.
> Blend rest of oil and the vinegar in a salad bowl. Add basil, mushrooms, ham, truffles and celery. Season to taste with salt and freshly ground black pepper. Toss thoroughly. Chill in refrigerator several hours before serving.

1

ANCHOVY AND EGGS

Serves 4

2   *tablespoons butter*
1   *heart of Bermuda onion, finely chopped*
6   *hard-boiled eggs, chopped*
4   *anchovy fillets, finely chopped*
     Small rounds of toast
     Sprigs of fresh parsley

> In a skillet melt butter and gently sauté onions until golden brown. Add eggs and heat thoroughly. Add anchovies and serve immediately on toast lightly sautéed in butter. Garnish with parsley.

ARTICHOKE HEARTS WITH ANCHOVIES AND CAPERS

READY TRAY   Serves 6 to 8

1   *jar (13 ounces) artichoke hearts*
4   *anchovy fillets, minced*
2   *teaspoons capers, minced*
1   *teaspoon lemon juice*
1   *tablespoon minced fresh parsley*
     Crackers

> Split the artichoke hearts and spoon out a few of the center leaves.
> Fill the cavities with the blended anchovies, capers and lemon juice. Garnish with minced parsley and chill thoroughly.
> Serve with crackers.

BAGNA CAUDA   Serves 4

This is a butter, olive oil, anchovy and garlic sauce which makes a tasty "warm bath" for crisp raw vegetables.

It is said to have originated with the peasants of Italy's Piedmont region in the foothills of the Alps, and was usually served in the dead of winter when the snows were deep. A credenza, or sideboard, would be moved to the center of the room and set with a bowl of Bagna cauda, surrounded by bowls containing cardone (an Italian chard or white cabbage picked in early fall and buried underground to be retrieved, when needed) and slices of red bell peppers (prepared in advance by marinating them for three months in wine mash). A large platter of homemade bread and bottles of red and white wine completed the table.

The invited guests would gather around the credenza. Then, holding a slice of bread in the left hand, each would take a piece of cardone or of bell pepper, dip it into the Bagna cauda with the right hand, bite into it (the cardone or pepper, not the hand) and almost simultaneously take a bite of bread. This would impregnate the bread with the juices of the Bagna cauda.

READY TRAY

4   *tablespoons butter*
14   *flat fillets of anchovy*
2   *large cloves of garlic, finely chopped*
8   *tablespoons olive oil*
2   *tablespoons red wine vinegar*
½   *medium-size head of white cabbage, finely shredded*
   Freshly ground black pepper
   Salt

Simmer butter in hot crepe pan over direct flame. When butter begins to brown, add garlic and brown lightly. Then add olive oil and anchovies. Heat thoroughly, and add red wine vinegar. Bring to a simmer and pour over shredded white cabbage. Toss well and season to taste with coarsely ground black pepper and a minimum amount of salt.

You prefer not to serve shredded cabbage? Simply put out celery stalks, finocchio (fennel), cardone or raw carrot sticks to dip into the succulent mixture.

CHICKEN LIVERS ON TOAST

READY TRAY   Serves 4

16   *chicken livers, halved and lightly floured*
3   *tablespoons butter*
4   *tablespoons dry white wine*
8   *fresh mushrooms, finely chopped*
   Salt and pepper
4   *slices trimmed bread, sautéed lightly in butter*
4   *sprigs fresh parsley*

3

In a skillet over high direct flame, sauté chicken livers in butter until browned and sealed on all sides. This will take about four minutes.

Add mushrooms, salt and freshly ground black pepper to taste, and simmer for three minutes.

Add wine, simmer for minute or two, and serve immediately on freshly sautéed bread. Garnish with parsley.

CHICKEN LIVERS AND ANCHOVIES ON TOAST

READY TRAY   Serves 2

6   *chicken livers*
4   *tablespoons butter*
    Chicken broth or hot water
    Freshly ground black pepper
6   *flat anchovy fillets*
    Trimmed triangles of toast

Cut chicken livers into small pieces and sauté in 2 tablespoons of butter until tender. If the livers become too dry, add a small amount of broth or hot water and blend thoroughly. Season to taste with pepper.

Place the livers and anchovies on a chopping board and chop together until very fine. Place in a small frying pan with 2 tablespoons butter. Mash and blend to a smooth paste over a very low flame.

Spread over toast while still warm, and serve.

CECI MARINARA

READY TRAY   Serves 6 to 8

2   *1-pound cans ceci beans (garbanzos)*
½   *cup olive oil*
1   *small can flat anchovy fillets, drained and finely chopped*
1   *teaspoon freshly ground black pepper*
2   *tablespoons fresh parsley, finely chopped*

Drain one can ceci. Combine with second can of undrained ceci, place in small saucepan and heat slowly.

Heat oil, add anchovies, pepper and parsley. Stir over

4

very low heat for a few minutes. Pour over heated ceci, mix thoroughly and simmer slowly for 15 minutes.

Serve hot or cold. Thoroughly chilled in this sauce, the ceci make a superb appetizer.

CLAM SCALLOP

READY TRAY   Serves 4

¼   *cup butter*
2   *tablespoons fresh green onions, finely chopped*
1   *tablespoon chopped fresh parsley*
1   *cup fresh clams, drained and minced*
⅓   *cup cream*
   Salt and pepper
   Paprika
1½   *cups buttered breadcrumbs*
   Scallop or clam shells or small pastry shells

Melt butter in top of double boiler. Add onions, parsley and clams and simmer for a few minutes. Add cream, salt, freshly ground black pepper to taste, a dash of paprika for color, and heat until cream is thoroughly heated. Sprinkle generously with buttered breadcrumbs.

Serve in scallop or clam shells or small pastry shells, or over crackers or small pieces of toast.

BEEF MARROW BORDELAISE ON TOAST

READY TRAY   Serves 2

20   *beef marrow bones, cut ½ inch thick*
1   *pint boiling water*
1   *teaspoon salt*
1   *tablespoon melted butter*
1   *whole fresh spring green onion, finely chopped*
1   *clove garlic, minced*
2   *tablespoons strained mushroom sauce*
   Salt and pepper (pepper heavy to taste)
2   *tablespoons red burgundy wine*
1   *tablespoon Cognac or brandy*
1   *tablespoon finely chopped parsley*
   Watercress
   Small triangles of toast

Remove eye of raw marrow from the bone by pressing gently. Place marrow in salted boiling water in a shallow pan, and boil for one minute. Remove marrow and put in strainer. Strain all water by shaking gently. Arrange marrow on toast and pour sauce over and garnish with watercress. Serve piping hot. This delicacy must be eaten immediately or it loses its savory taste.

Sauce: Simmer butter in small skillet over direct heat and while it is bubbling, add chopped onions and garlic. Sauté until golden brown. Add mushroom sauce and season to taste with salt and pepper. Add wine and Cognac or brandy, blend thoroughly and sprinkle with parsley.

EGGPLANT SPREAD

(CAPONATA)

READY TRAY   Serves 6

1   large eggplant, peeled and cubed
4   tablespoons olive oil
½   can tomato sauce (8-ounce size)
1   small carrot, finely chopped
2   stalks celery, finely chopped
2   teaspoons capers, finely chopped
1   tablespoon wine vinegar
1   bay leaf
½   teaspoon oregano
½   teaspoon salt
     Freshly ground black pepper to taste

Sauté cubed eggplant in oil until just tender and set aside. Combine the tomato sauce, carrot, celery and capers and cook until vegetables are tender. Add vinegar, bay leaf, oregano, salt and pepper and eggplant to the sauce. Simmer gently for 15 minutes until thoroughly blended. Cool thoroughly before serving on crackers or small pieces of toast.

FONDUE PIEMONTESE

When the peasants in the "old country" could afford the price of a truffle and the ingredients for a feast, everyone stood around the table, elbows and hands moving in all

6

directions, dunking bread into the bubbling cheese sauce in an earthenware casserole placed in the center of the table. The first one to sit down, too filled with fondue and red wine to continue, was disqualified and could not go back for seconds.

Servings Optional

4   *tablespoons butter*
1   *pound imported fontina cheese, diced*
½   *pound fresh creamy ricotta cheese*
1   *cup white sauterne wine*
1   *egg yolk*
1   *whole Italian white truffle, sliced tissue thin*
    Freshly ground black pepper
    Homemade bread or Italian bread

Melt butter in a double boiler over a very high flame, or in a fondue pan. Add cheeses and blend, by stirring or whipping with a wire whisk. When cheeses are thoroughly melted, add the wine and pepper to taste and simmer 5 minutes. Before serving, blend in the egg yolk and place truffle slices on top of the fondue.

To serve, keep the fondue pan over a low flame. Fill a basket with bite-size pieces of bread. Let your guests help themselves and dunk the bread into the fondue.

MAMA'S GREEN BEANS

READY TRAY   Serves 8

2   *pounds fresh string beans, cut in 2-inch lengths*
1   *cup water in which beans were cooked*
3   *tablespoons olive oil*
2   *tablespoons fresh lemon juice*
1   *teaspoon dill weed*
½   *teaspoon fresh basil, finely chopped*
1   *garlic clove, peeled*
    Salt
    Freshly ground black pepper

Cover beans with salted water and cook until tender. Drain, reserving 1 cup liquid, and cool thoroughly.

Combine the reserved liquid, oil, lemon juice, dill weed, basil, garlic; season to taste with salt and freshly ground black pepper and blend thoroughly. Pour over the beans and marinate several hours or overnight in refrigerator before serving.

Any cooked dried beans of your choice may be prepared in this manner. The beans should be soaked overnight before cooking to plump them up.

MELON AND PROSCIUTTO

READY TRAY   Serves 4

1   *melon, your choice, chilled*
    Prosciutto, thinly sliced

Cut each melon half into 4 or 6 wedges. Carefully wrap a thin slice of prosciutto around each wedge, and serve.

Fresh peeled figs or drained canned figs may also be prepared in this manner.

MARINATED MUSHROOMS

READY TRAY   Serves 6

1   *pound whole fresh mushrooms, small size*
4   *tablespoons wine vinegar*
3   *tablespoons olive oil*
½   *teaspoon salt*
½   *teaspoon oregano*
    Dash freshly ground black pepper
1   *tablespoon chopped fresh parsley*
1   *clove garlic, gently crushed*

Wash mushrooms and cook in a small amount of boiling salted water until slightly tender, approximately 5 to 10 minutes. Drain thoroughly.
Blend remaining ingredients thoroughly and pour over the mushrooms. Marinate in refrigerator several hours before serving.

This marinade may be used to pickle cooked arti-

choke hearts, cauliflower, green beans or garbanzo beans
with the addition of a little chopped onion.

OLIVES

Green and black olives (pitted or unpitted) may be served
as antipasto as they come from the containers in which they
are packed.

A great variety of Italian olives of pleasing and different
tastes may be purchased at any Italian delicatessen.

If unpitted green olives are used, prepare them in the
following way.

READY TRAY   Servings Optional

1 No. 2½ can green olives
2 cloves garlic, chopped fine
2 tablespoons fresh parsley, chopped fine
2 tablespoons olive oil

Drain the olives and crush them with a wooden mallet
until the pulp is gently broken, being careful not to
crack the pit.

Place olives in a bowl, add garlic, parsley and oil. Mix
thoroughly and marinate several hours before serving,
stirring the olives every half hour. The longer the olives
remain in the marinade, the more flavorful they become.

PEPERONCINI

(PRESERVED PEPPERS)

READY TRAY   Serves 6 to 8

1 6-ounce can or jar peperoncini peppers in vinegar
1 clove garlic, gently crushed
3 tablespoons olive oil
1 tablespoon wine vinegar

Drain peperoncini and snip off the small ends to drain
off the juice that has penetrated the peppers. Leave the
stems on for handling.

Place the peppers in a bowl and add garlic. Blend oil
and vinegar and pour over the peppers to cover.

Marinate for several hours before serving.

9

PIZZA

Pizza was originally made from boiled polenta (cornmeal) which was poured out onto a wooden slab and covered with tomato sauce. What was not eaten at its first serving was allowed to cool. Then it was cut into squares, the squares sprinkled with cheese and toasted before serving.

It was the Neapolitans who came up with the idea of using a raised bread dough instead of the polenta for the pizza. As for the sauces, there are as many variations as there are towns and villages in Italy.

Pizza makes a piquant, thirst-provoking, savory appetizer —excellent for convivial occasions and popular with everyone.

READY TRAY   Servings Optional

Pizza Dough

1	cake or package yeast
1	cup lukewarm water
3¼	cups sifted flour
¼	teaspoon salt
2	tablespoons shortening
½	cup olive oil

READY TRAY

Filling

1	onion, finely chopped
1	cup grated Parmesan cheese
	or
	Thin slices mozzarella cheese
4	ripe tomatoes, peeled and chopped
	or
1	small can Italian tomato puree, diluted with broth
	or
1	cup prepared tomato sauce
1	clove garlic, finely chopped
	Freshly ground black pepper
½	teaspoon basil
½	teaspoon marjoram
12	anchovy fillets, coarsely chopped
12	pitted black olives

Soak yeast in lukewarm water 5 minutes. Combine flour and salt, add shortening and blend until crumbly. Add yeast mixture and knead until smooth and elastic.

10

Form into ball, place in greased bowl, cover and let rise in warm place for 2 hours.

Divide dough into 2 equal parts and roll or stretch out to a ¼-inch thickness. Shape into round or oblong pizzas, about 10 to 12 inches across, or larger, if you wish.

Gently heat one-half of the oil in the baking dish. Place rolled-out dough into baking dish, cover with cloth, set aside in warm place, away from drafts, to rise 20 to 30 minutes.

Sauté onions in oil until transparent. Sprinkle lightly over raised dough. Spread grated cheese or place sliced mozzarella cheese evenly over onions. Add tomatoes or sauce over cheese. Sprinkle with garlic, pepper to taste, basil and marjoram. Arrange anchovies and olives over top and pour remainder of oil over all to coat.

Bake in 350° oven for 20 to 30 minutes until bottom of pizza is crisp and brown, and top is bubbly.

Cut into small squares, triangles or pie-shaped wedges to serve.

Sliced ham, salami or sausages are also used for pizza.

PIZZA
(Shortcut method)

Here is a quick and easy way to prepare a tasty pizza, using a hot roll mix. Prepare pizza dough as directed on the package. But ignore directions that read, "Do not raise dough for pizza." The dough should be raised *once*.

READY TRAY

Pizza Dough

1	package hot roll mix
¼	cup Parmesan cheese
¼	cup olive oil

Filling

1	can Italian-style plum tomatoes (1 pound 1 ounce)
1	tablespoon oregano
1	clove garlic
1	teaspoon sugar
	Salt to taste
¼	cup Parmesan cheese

Cook together ingredients for filling for 15 minutes.

11

Remove garlic, correct for salt. Set aside to cool while dough raises.

Place olive oil in bottom of 9 x 14 baking pan. Stretch the raised dough to fit the pan comfortably; the olive oil will cover the top of the dough as well. Ladle tomato sauce over the dough evenly, and sprinkle Parmesan cheese over it.

Bake in 350° oven for 20 to 30 minutes until done.

SCAMPI

READY TRAY   Serves 4 to 6

   2   *pounds fresh shrimp with shells*
   4   *tablespoons butter*
   4   *tablespoons olive oil*
  ⅓   *cup white wine*
   1   *tablespoon parsley, finely chopped*
  ½   *teaspoon fresh basil, finely chopped*
  ½   *teaspoon fresh oregano, finely chopped*
       Salt and pepper
   1   *tablespoon lemon juice*

Clean shrimp; remove shells but leave tail intact.

Heat butter and oil in frying pan. Add wine, using more if desired, parsley, basil, oregano, salt and pepper to taste. Heat thoroughly. Add shrimp and sauté quickly until shrimp begin to take on color, 2 or 3 minutes. Sprinkle with lemon juice before serving.

Serve with crusty slices of Italian bread to soak up the juices. Two or three shrimp are sufficient as an appetizer.

MARINATED SQUID
(CALAMARI)

READY TRAY   Serves 4 to 6

   1   *pound squid*
          or
   1   *pound small fresh fish, your choice*
       Flour
       Olive oil
       Salt and pepper
   1   *clove garlic, finely chopped*
   1   *sprig fresh rosemary*
   1   *cup white wine vinegar*

Clean squid by cutting off the heads and removing the bone and food tubes. Wash out the ink and skin them by pulling the skin at the fins. (They skin easily.) Cut the meat into ½-inch slices. Flour lightly and fry in oil until golden brown on all sides. Drain on absorbent paper, place in a bowl and season to taste with salt and pepper.

Brown garlic and rosemary in 2 tablespoons of olive oil, add vinegar and bring to a boil. Cool and pour over squid. Marinate several hours before serving.

Small fish, no larger than 8 inches, may be prepared and marinated in this same way. If kept in a cool place, they will keep for several days. When using large fish, be sure to fillet them and cut into bite-size pieces.

MARINATED TUNA WITH ANCHOVIES

READY TRAY   Serves 6

1   6-ounce can tuna fish
1   tablespoon olive oil
1   clove garlic, finely chopped
1   fresh spring green onion, finely chopped
2   anchovy fillets, finely chopped
    Juice of ½ lemon
    Freshly ground black pepper
    Crackers or small triangles of toast

Drain oil from tuna. Place in a bowl and mash gently with a fork.

Add the oil, garlic, onion, anchovies, lemon juice, and pepper to taste. Blend thoroughly.

Serve on crackers or toast.

GARLIC MAYONNAISE TOAST

READY TRAY   Serves 4

1   cup mayonnaise
½   cup grated Parmesan cheese
4   fresh green onions, finely chopped
½   teaspoon garlic powder
1   loaf Italian bread, cut lengthwise, then cut
     to crust, in 1½-inch slices

13

Blend the mayonnaise, cheese, onions and garlic powder until smooth.

Spread thickly over the bread and place under the broiler until delicately browned.

This toast may also be served with the salad or soup courses, and is excellent with main entrées.

GARLIC CHEESE TOAST

READY TRAY   Serves 4

¼ *pound butter*
1 *cup grated Parmesan cheese*
1 *tablespoon garlic powder*
1 *loaf Italian bread, split down the center and cut into 3-inch slices*
   Paprika

Melt butter in top of double boiler, then blend well with cheese and garlic powder. Ladle onto each slice of bread enough of the cheese mixture to cover the surface completely. Keep stirring the mixture in the double boiler as you work.

Place the bread pieces 4 inches below direct flame of the broiler. Remove when the center of the cheese-covered slices begin to have a golden-brown color. Sprinkle with paprika for color, or with garniture, and serve hot.

This toast may also be made with melted butter and finely chopped garlic, omitting the cheese, if desired, and browned in the same manner.

Soups

The soup we associate with Italian cuisine is the *minestra*. This is a thin soup made from boiled beef, veal or chicken, flavored and enriched by adding fresh vegetables in season, a dry cereal or both.

When these ingredients are used abundantly or are heavier, like dried beans, then the soup becomes the hearty, thick *minestrone*, which can be a meal in itself. Serve only a small cup as a soup course.

For a lighter start to dinner, a clear broth is preferable. Adding tiny pasta or custard balls gives a broth a different, "angelic" flavor.

What gives all Italian soups, thick or thin, their unmistakable character is the lavish use of grated Parmesan cheese, stirred into the soup to thicken it or served separately at the table.

Many of the recipes in this section call for broth. *Broth, bouillon* or *stock*—the terms are interchangeable. Served as it comes from the soup pot, broth is the clear liquid to which a simple garnish such as rice, thin noodles or vermicelli can be added. Stock is this same liquid used in making sauces or more elaborate soups—brown stock if made from beef, white if made from chicken or veal. Consommé is broth made richer by using extra meat and chicken, and clarified by adding lightly beaten egg whites.

Preparation of Broth or Stock

Meaty beef bones, a plump fowl, or chicken and beef together make excellent basic stocks.

For more flavor brown the beef bones in a shallow roasting pan. Then place them in a 4- to 6-quart soup kettle, and cover with cold water. Add a little salt because this helps extract flavor from the meat, but wait until the stock is almost ready to serve before seasoning fully to taste.

For flavor, wash and tie together a few sticks of celery, leeks, carrots, parsley and fresh basil—a bouquet garni. It's a good idea to remove and discard this during the cooking period before it becomes overcooked.

As the liquid heats, a foam or scum will rise to the surface of the kettle. As it forms, remove this scum carefully with a large spoon. When the liquid begins to boil, stir it a little to make the last of the scum rise quickly. Then reduce heat, cover the kettle and let simmer several hours undisturbed. Stirring it now will cause the stock to be cloudy. When the cooking period is over, ladle out as much as possible of the liquid without disturbing the solid ingredients. This stock will be very clear.

Cool stock uncovered at room temperature before refrigerating.

15

Some further pointers: If you intend to serve the boiled meat as a course, then bring the water to a boil before adding the meat. This seals the surfaces of the meat and preserves the good meat flavors.

When freezing extra soup, *do not add pasta*. Add it when the soup is reheated because pasta does not freeze well.

ANGELIC SOUP

READY TRAY   Serves 4

6   tablespoons fine breadcrumbs
5   cups broth
2   tablespoons prosciutto, finely chopped
2   tablespoons beef marrow, finely chopped
2   tablespoons grated Parmesan cheese
1   raw egg
⅛   teaspoon grated nutmeg
    Flour

Put breadcrumbs in a bowl and add enough broth to moisten them slightly. Add prosciutto, marrow, cheese, egg and nutmeg to the breadcrumbs and blend thoroughly.

Sprinkle a little flour on a breadboard, place this mixture on it and work into a medium-hard dough, adding flour as needed to maintain firmness of dough. Roll out to ½-inch thickness and cut into ½-inch squares; roll these into balls and drop into the boiling broth. Cook for 5 minutes over medium heat.

Serve hot in individual bowls. More grated cheese may be sprinkled over the soup to taste.

EGG SOUP

READY TRAY   Serves 6

6   eggs
2   teaspoons flour
6   cups broth
2   tablespoons fresh parsley, finely chopped
3   tablespoons grated Parmesan cheese
    Salt and pepper

Beat eggs, add flour slowly and whip together until light. Bring broth to a boil and slowly add the egg mixture, stirring gently with a large spoon. If the egg flakes appear too large, add a little lukewarm broth to the mixture and blend thoroughly. Simmer gently for 5 minutes.

Add parsley, cheese, salt and pepper to taste, and serve immediately in hot soup plates.

ANGELIC SOUP WITH CHICKEN

READY TRAY   Serves 4 to 6

1   breast of chicken, cut into 1-inch pieces
4   tablespoons butter
6   cups broth
    Salt and pepper
2   egg yolks, beaten lightly
6   slices bread, trimmed and diced
    Dash of freshly grated nutmeg
    Flour

Sauté chicken breast in butter over low heat. If it becomes dry, add a little broth and continue cooking until chicken is tender, approximately 20 minutes. Season to taste with salt and pepper.

Remove chicken from pan. Add beaten egg yolks and diced bread to liquid remaining in pan, adding broth, if needed, to maintain a thick mixture; blend until smooth. Add sautéed chicken and nutmeg, blend thoroughly. Remove from heat and put through fine grinder.

When cool, place on floured mixing board and roll out to ½-inch thickness. Cut into ½-inch squares and roll into small balls.

Bring remaining broth to a gentle boil and drop in a few balls at a time, allowing the broth to continue boiling. Ready to serve in approximately 5 minutes.

BROTH WITH PASTA

Any of the small pastas may be used in this soup. A few varieties are alphabet, pastina, stars, little shells, little tubes, noodles, spaghettini and capellini. The last three must be broken into shorter lengths.

17

4   cups broth
1   cup pasta, your choice
*   Salt and pepper*
4   tablespoons grated Parmesan cheese
1   tablespoon parsley, chopped fine

      Bring broth to a boil and slowly drop the pasta into it, stirring gently to prevent sticking. The length of cooking time depends on the thickness of the pasta, generally from 6 to 12 minutes. To tell when it is done to suit your taste, bite into one of the pieces of pasta. From this practice is derived the expression *al dente* or "to the teeth." When the pasta feels tender to you, it is ready. Season the broth to taste with salt and pepper. Serve in individual soup bowls and garnish with grated cheese and parsley.

      Note: For a reddish color, add a tablespoon of diluted tomato paste or tomato sauce to the stock while it is heating. For a golden color, add a small pinch of saffron.

CECI BEAN MINESTRA

½   cup olive oil
½   teaspoon rosemary
1   clove garlic, finely chopped
3   anchovy fillets, finely chopped
1   tablespoon tomato paste
4   tablespoons water
1   cup cooked ceci beans (garbanzos)
4   cups water
*   Salt and pepper*
1   cup elbow macaroni
*   Grated Parmesan cheese*

      Place oil, rosemary and garlic in soup kettle and brown well. Add anchovies and tomato paste diluted with 4 tablespoons water and cook over low heat 20 minutes.
      Add ceci beans, water, salt and pepper, and bring to a slow boil.

Add macaroni and cook slowly until tender, approximately 15 minutes.
Garnish with cheese when ready to serve.

FRESH CLAM SOUP

READY TRAY   Serves 4

3   *pounds fresh clams in shells*
1   *onion, finely chopped*
2   *cloves garlic, finely chopped*
2   *stalks celery, finely chopped*
2   *tablespoons parsley, finely chopped*
3   *tablespoons olive oil*
1   *ounce dried mushrooms, soaked, drained and finely chopped*
    Salt and pepper
4   *slices buttered toast, cut in ½-inch cubes*

Place clams in fresh water to cover, with one tablespoon salt, and soak for several hours. Remove clams from water, scrub and drain well. Put them in a large kettle in 4 cups of cold water, cover and place over medium heat. As soon as the shells begin to open, remove from heat, pick the meat out of the shells and set aside. Let liquid sit for a few minutes, then strain through a clean cloth.

Sauté onion, garlic, celery and parsley lightly in oil. Add mushrooms and ½ cup hot water; cook over low heat until celery is tender.

Add clam broth and clam meat, and salt and pepper to taste. When soup comes to a boil, remove from heat. Garnish with toast cubes and serve.

REGINA SOUP

READY TRAY   Serves 4

4   *egg yolks*
6   *tablespoons flour*
4   *tablespoons grated Parmesan cheese*
6   *cups broth*
    Salt and pepper

19

Beat egg yolks until light. Add flour and cheese and blend to a smooth, thin batter. Correct thickness with broth or flour, as necessary for smoothness.

Bring broth to a boil. Place round-bottomed colander on top of the broth kettle, then pour the batter into the colander and force it down slowly into the broth so that the batter emerges in the form of spaghetti. It should not require much force to push the batter through the colander. Boil gently for 8 minutes. Season to taste with salt and pepper before serving.

MINESTRONE ALLA NORTH BEACH, SAN FRANCISCO

READY TRAY   Serves 6

1   cup dried white beans, or 3 cups cooked beans
¼   pound salt pork
3   leeks, cut in ¼-inch pieces
9   cups broth
1   small head cabbage, curly variety preferred, cut into ½-inch strips
2   tablespoons parsley, finely chopped
3   stalks celery, chopped
1   potato, peeled and diced in ½-inch cubes
1   tablespoon tomato paste, diluted with a little broth
    Salt
    Freshly ground black pepper
½   cup macaroni (ditalini)
    Grated Parmesan cheese

Cook beans in water to cover, approximately 3 hours, before starting the Minestrone. Grind or chop salt pork fine and render well, over low heat. Strain through a fine sieve or cloth and put the fat in a large soup kettle. Add leeks and wilt.

Bring broth to a boil and add to leeks. Add cabbage, parsley, celery, potato, tomato paste, and season to taste with salt and pepper. Cover and cook over medium heat until vegetables are tender, approximately 45 minutes. Add the macaroni 15 minutes before the minestrone is ready.

Put two-thirds of the cooked beans through a sieve, add to minestrone and blend thoroughly. Add balance of the whole beans. If the soup is too thick, add more broth.

Serve hot and pass the cheese!

MUSHROOM SOUP

Serves 4

2   tablespoons finely chopped salt pork
2   tablespoons butter
1   tablespoon olive oil
1   tablespoon finely chopped parsley
1   pound fresh mushrooms, washed, drained and finely chopped
    Salt and pepper
6   cups broth
1   egg
1   tablespoon grated Parmesan cheese
4   slices toast, cut into small cubes

> Sauté salt pork lightly in butter and oil, add parsley, mushrooms, and salt and pepper to taste and cook for 2 minutes. Bring broth to a boil and add the sautéed ingredients, cooking gently until the mushrooms are tender.
>
> In a soup tureen beat the egg with the cheese. Pour the hot soup into the tureen, stirring gently. Serve in individual soup plates and garnish with the toasted cubes.

PAPA'S PASTA E FAGIOLI
(FROM A 2,000-YEAR-OLD RECIPE)

READY TRAY   Serves 6 to 8

1   pound white dried beans, soaked in water to cover
     Salt
1   cup olive oil
1   clove garlic, unpeeled
1   large-leaf Italian bay leaf
1   teaspoon coarsely ground hot red pepper
     Few sprigs parsley
½   pound salad macaroni
     Grated Parmesan cheese

> Cook beans in water in which they were soaked. Salt to taste, bring to slow boil, skim foam, add oil, garlic and bay leaf. Cook beans gently until tender, approximately 2 hours. The oil will be completely absorbed and a delicate flavor is the result. Remove garlic and bay leaf.
>
> Cook the macaroni, drain and reserve 1 cup of liquid.

21

Add pasta to the beans, with the reserved liquid and the hot pepper, and simmer until thick.

Garnish with parsley and grated cheese before serving.

TOMATO SOUP SUPREME

READY TRAY   Serves 4 to 6

1   No. 2½ can tomatoes, well mashed
1   onion, finely chopped
1   carrot, finely chopped
2   stalks celery, thinly sliced
2   tablespoons parsley, finely chopped
6   cups broth
    Salt and pepper
8   tablespoons butter
6   slices bread, trimmed and cut in 1-inch squares
    Grated Parmesan cheese

Combine all the vegetables and add to boiling broth. Season to taste with salt and pepper. Cover and simmer slowly, approximately 1½ hours. Then force everything through a sieve. Return the liquid to the heat, add the butter and simmer slowly for 5 minutes.

Sauté bread squares lightly in butter. Place in soup tureen and pour hot tomato soup over them. Serve in individual soup plates. Pass grated cheese separately.

EXQUISITE SOUP

READY TRAY   Serves 6

4   eggs, separated
4   tablespoons breadcrumbs
4   tablespoons grated Parmesan cheese
    Dash grated nutmeg
    Salt
6   cups broth

Beat egg whites until stiff and fold into lightly beaten egg yolks. Add breadcrumbs, cheese, nutmeg and salt to taste. Blend until smooth.

Bring broth to a gentle boil. Drop above mixture, a

22

half-teaspoonful at a time, into broth and cook gently, approximately 7 minutes. Serve in hot soup plates.

LEAF VEGETABLE SOUP

READY TRAY

Any one of the following leaf vegetables:
Escarole
Endive
Chicory
Chard
Dandelion
Mustard greens
Spinach
Radichetti

Any one of these leaf vegetables, boiled and drained, makes a delicious plain vegetable soup.

Place a small quantity of the vegetable of your choice, already boiled and drained, in individual soup plates. Pour over some hot rich broth, sprinkle with grated Parmesan or Romano cheese—and you have antipasto, soup and salad in one! The next dish served is the main entrée.

WEDDING SOUP
(MARITATA)

READY TRAY   Serves 4 to 6

1½   *quarts strained rich chicken broth*
½   *pound ground beef*
½   *pound ground veal or pork*
1   *egg*
½   *cup breadcrumbs*
1   *teaspoon salt*
½   *teaspoon black pepper*
1½   *tablespoons parsley, finely chopped*
¼   *cup broth*
      Lard
1   *cup pastina*

This soup is generally served at weddings and feasts.

Blend thoroughly the meat, egg, breadcrumbs, salt, pepper, parsley and ¼ cup broth. Shape into marble-size balls with your hands. Brown in lard and drain on absorbent paper.

Bring broth to a boil, add the pastina and cook until pastina is tender. Drop in the meatballs and cook for 10 minutes until thoroughly heated.

Homemade noodle dough may be substituted for the pastina. Blend until smooth, 2 eggs with 2 cups flour and 1 tablespoon water. Roll dough into pencil-size strips and cut into pea-size pieces. Deep-fry pieces in lard. Drain thoroughly and drop into hot chicken broth with the meatballs. Cook slowly for 20 minutes before serving.

MINESTRONE

READY TRAY   Serves 6

1   small head cabbage, curly variety preferred
¼   pound spinach
¼   pound Swiss chard
2   beets with leaves
2   stalks celery
1   carrot
1   large potato
1   zucchini
1   onion
1   cup fresh or frozen peas
8   cups beef broth
⅛   pound prosciutto, finely chopped
1   clove garlic, finely chopped
2   tablespoons parsley, finely chopped
     Olive oil
⅓   cup uncooked rice
     Salt and pepper
     Grated Parmesan cheese

Wash vegetables thoroughly and drain. Shred into ½-inch pieces the cabbage, spinach, chard and beet leaves. Dice into ½-inch pieces the celery, carrot, potato, zucchini, onion and beets. Bring broth to a boil, turn heat down to medium, add the shredded and diced vegetables and the peas.

Sauté prosciutto, garlic and parsley lightly in oil in a saucepan. Add with rice to the cooking vegetables. Season

24

to taste with salt and pepper. Cook over medium heat for 30 minutes until rice and vegetables are tender.

Serve with grated cheese and crusty pieces of Italian bread.

POTATO BALL SOUP

READY TRAY   Serves 6

1½   *pounds potatoes*
3   *egg yolks*
6   *tablespoons grated Parmesan cheese*
8   *tablespoons butter*
      Salt and pepper
      Flour
      Olive oil
8   *cups broth*
2   *tablespoons parsley, finely chopped*

Boil potatoes with skins until tender. Peel and pass through a sieve into a bowl. Add egg yolks, cheese, butter, and salt and pepper to taste. Blend thoroughly.

Place mixture on a floured mixing board and roll to ½-inch thickness. Cut into ½-inch squares, form into balls and roll lightly in flour.

Brown potato balls a few at a time in hot oil. Keep warm in a soup tureen. When all the potato balls are ready, pour boiling broth over them and serve in individual soup plates. Garnish with chopped parsley.

LENTIL AND PASTINA SOUP

READY TRAY   Serves 6 to 8

¾   *cup dried lentils*
2   *slices bacon, cut in small squares*
1   *onion, thinly sliced*
2   *cloves garlic, finely chopped*
4   *large tomatoes, peeled and quartered*
1   *stalk celery, coarsely chopped*
     Salt
     Freshly ground black pepper
     Pinch dried mint leaves
1   *2-ounce package pastina*

25

Cover lentils with cold water and soak for 2 hours. Drain and place in a large soup kettle.

Render bacon and in the fat sauté the onion, garlic, tomatoes and celery for 5 minutes, stirring constantly.

Add to lentils and stir until they have absorbed the remaining bacon fat. Season with salt and pepper and mint leaves.

Add 7 cups hot water and cook over medium-high heat for 1 hour. Add pastina and cook gently for 15 minutes.

Serve hot with crusty Italian bread.

FISH SOUP

READY TRAY   Serves 4 to 6

2   *pounds sea fish, rather fat*
    Salt and pepper
1   *bay leaf*
1   *onion, finely chopped*
1   *carrot, finely chopped*
2   *cloves garlic, finely chopped*
2   *stalks celery, finely chopped*
4   *tablespoons olive oil*
1   *ounce dried mushrooms, soaked in hot water, strained and finely chopped*
1   *tablespoon tomato paste, diluted in a little broth*
4   *slices toasted bread, cut in ½-inch cubes*
2   *tablespoons grated Parmesan cheese*
    Lemon wedges

Clean fish thoroughly and cut in serving-size pieces. Place in large kettle, cover with water and season to taste with salt and pepper. Add bay leaf, bring to boil and simmer gently for 15 minutes. Strain liquid from fish. Keep fish warm on the side.

Sauté onion, carrot, garlic and celery lightly in oil. Add mushrooms, diluted tomato paste and strained fish stock. Cover and simmer slowly for 20 minutes or until vegetables and mushrooms are tender.

Serve in individual soup bowls and garnish with cheese and toasted bread cubes.

If desired, fish can be served as an entreé, with lemon wedges.

Salads

Crisp, chilled greens flavored with fresh or dried herbs and sprinkled lightly with oil, vinegar, salt, freshly ground black pepper and a gentle hint of garlic—that is the Italian salad in its purest form. If a saltier taste is preferred, blend mashed anchovies into the dressing, omitting the salt.

Fresh herbs such as basil, chervil, tarragon, oregano, parsley and many others can be used more generously than dried herbs because of their milder flavor, and are best when chopped finely, to allow their distinctive flavors to permeate the salad bowl. Or add grated Parmesan cheese for that extra flavor; the salty tang of the cheese doesn't overpower but blends well with and brings out other flavors.

When to serve the salad? As the antipasto course, after the main course to clear the palate, with the main course or as the main course. It's up to you!

CAESAR SALAD

The Caesar Salad is said to have been named after a certain Caesar Cardini, a dining-room caterer working in Agua Caliente, and his partner. To the Bagna cauda sauce (see Antipasto chapter), they added a coddled egg, Parmesan cheese and a touch of Tabasco sauce. Served with a certain showmanship, it is today one of the most popular Italian salads served in American restaurants.

READY TRAY   Serves 2

2   *cloves garlic, peeled*
8   *croutons, ¾-inch cubes, well toasted*
8   *anchovy fillets*
1   *fresh whole egg, coddled*
1   *fresh lemon*
½   *teaspoon dry mustard*
1   *tablespoon Worcestershire sauce*
1   *tablespoon wine vinegar*
4   *tablespoons olive oil*
3   *drops Tabasco sauce*
4   *tablespoons grated Parmesan cheese*
1   *head romaine, iceberg or butter lettuce, torn in bite-size pieces*
1   *teaspoon freshly ground black pepper*

27

Use a large wooden bowl that is very dry. Place garlic cloves in bowl and mash, using prongs of a fork. Sprinkle mashed garlic lightly with salt. Now press the garlic fibers and juice into the wood, using the bowl of a large metal spoon in a rotary motion. Add a few croutons to the bowl, stirring them around delicately to capture the garlic flavor on the surface of the bowl. Then set croutons aside for use later.

Add 6 anchovy fillets and mince. Add coddled egg. Squeeze lemon, straining juice into bowl through napkin to hold back pulp and seeds. Then add dry mustard, Worcestershire sauce, vinegar, oil and Tabasco sauce. Sprinkle 3 tablespoons of cheese on the surface of dressing and whip it with a fork into a good consistency. Add the greens, making sure they are well dried and chilled. Toss well but do not bruise. Sprinkle with desired amount of freshly ground black pepper and toss lightly again.

Sprinkle remaining tablespoon of cheese on surface of salad and toss until every green leaf glistens with the dressing. To prevent croutons from becoming soggy, add them at the last moment. Serve on well-chilled salad plates, with 2 anchovy fillets in an X design over the salad.

Served with cheese or garlic toast, this is a good luncheon dish on a warm summer day.

TOMATO ANCHOVY SALAD

READY TRAY   Serves 4

8	center leaves romaine lettuce
8	slices ripe tomato, ½ inch thick, peeled and seeded
8	anchovy fillets
½	cup olive oil
¼	cup wine vinegar
	Freshly ground black pepper

Place romaine leaves on individual cold salad plates. Arrange 2 tomato slices on each plate, and top each slice with an anchovy fillet.

Blend thoroughly oil, vinegar and pepper to taste and sprinkle lightly over salad. Salt is omitted because the anchovy fillets are salty, but may be added to individual taste.

28

MAMA ROSSI'S SALAD

Serves 2

1   cup butter lettuce, torn into bite-size pieces
6   strips salami
6   strips cheese, your choice
2   anchovies, chopped
1   tablespoon olive oil
1   tablespoon wine vinegar
    Pinch of oregano
    Salt
    Freshly ground black pepper
2   slices Italian bread
2   Italian sausages, sliced and browned in wine (see Sausages in Wine)

> In a wooden salad bowl, toss lightly the lettuce, salami, cheese and anchovies.
> Blend oil, vinegar, oregano, salt and pepper to taste. Pour over salad and toss lightly.
> Serve in mounds over bread with sausages. This is a good luncheon dish.

ITALIAN POTATO SALAD

Serves 4

4   potatoes, cooked, peeled and diced
2   stalks celery, finely chopped
1   small cucumber, peeled and diced
½   cup ripe olives, pitted and sliced
2   tablespoons onion, finely chopped
6   tablespoons olive oil
3   tablespoons wine vinegar
1   clove garlic, gently crushed
¼   teaspoon oregano
    Salt
    Freshly ground black pepper

> Place potatoes in a large bowl and add the celery, cucumber, olives and onion, and toss together lightly.
> Blend oil, vinegar, crushed garlic, oregano, salt and pepper to taste until salt is dissolved. Pour over salad and blend carefully. Cover salad bowl and chill in refrigerator for several hours before serving.

29

CUCUMBER AND RICOTTA SALAD

Serves 4

2   cucumbers
1   cup ricotta cheese
1   tablespoon chives, finely chopped
1   small head lettuce, torn in bite-size pieces
¼   cup thinly sliced white radishes
¼   cup thinly sliced firm green pepper
8   Italian ripe olives
1   2-ounce can rolled anchovies with capers
1   tablespoon red wine vinegar
    Salt and pepper

Peel cucumbers and cut in half lengthwise. Scrape seeds from cucumbers, leaving oval shells.

Mix ricotta and chives, and spoon mixture into cucumber shells. Sprinkle with salt and set aside.

Place torn lettuce in salad bowl; add radishes, pepper slices, olives, anchovies with their oil and vinegar. Add additional olive oil if needed. Season to taste with salt and pepper and toss lightly.

Spoon salad mixture onto cold serving plates and place filled cucumber shells on top.

FLAMING SPINACH SALAD

Serves 4 to 6

1½   pounds fresh young tender spinach
½   pound bacon, diced
½   cup red wine vinegar
3   tablespoons Worcestershire sauce
1   juicy lemon (cut in half and squeezed through
     napkin to hold back seeds and pulp)
½   cup sugar
¼   cup Cognac or brandy

Remove stems from spinach leaves and discard. Wash leaves thoroughly and pat dry with clean cloth. Chill in refrigerator before using.

Sauté bacon in chafing dish over high flame until it just begins to brown. Add vinegar, Worcestershire sauce, lemon juice and sugar. Stir well until sugar is dissolved.

When sauce begins to simmer, pour it over fresh young tender spinach leaves, holding back diced bacon pieces in pan. Don't be afraid of bruising the leaves but toss briskly so dressing will penetrate as well as coat each tender leaf. Divide spinach evenly on salad plates, and set aside.

While chafing dish is heating and bacon pieces are browning, add Cognac or brandy with left hand, holding chafing dish with right hand. Be careful to pull pan back toward you 3 to 8 inches above flame. While bacon is still flaming, ladle it evenly over the individual mounds of spinach on salad plates and serve immediately.

No salt or pepper is to be used or added because it will take away from the proper enjoyment of the full-bodied sweet and sour flavor. So warn your guests!

FENNEL SALAD

READY TRAY   Serves 6

1   clove garlic
1   head fennel, thinly sliced
1   head chicory, torn in bite-size pieces
2   large fresh tomatoes, cut in wedges
    Salt
    Freshly ground black pepper
6   tablespoons olive oil
2   tablespoons wine vinegar

Rub the inside of a large salad bowl with garlic. Add fennel, chicory, tomatoes, salt and pepper to taste.

Blend the oil and vinegar and pour over the salad. Toss thoroughly and serve immediately.

ESCAROLE SALAD

READY TRAY   Serves 4

1   medium head escarole, torn into bite-size pieces
3   tablespoons olive oil
1   tablespoon tarragon vinegar
1   teaspoon fresh sweet basil, finely chopped
    Salt
    Freshly ground black pepper

31

Place escarole in a wooden salad bowl. Blend oil, vinegar, basil, salt and pepper to taste. Pour over greens and toss gently.

Serve on individual chilled salad plates.

Romaine, chicory, and all varieties of lettuce may be treated in the same way.

TOMATO GARLIC SALAD

READY TRAY   Serves 1

3   *center leaves romaine lettuce*
1   *ripe tomato, peeled, seeded and cut in 4 slices*
1   *small clove garlic, finely chopped*
3   *tablespoons olive oil*
1   *tablespoon wine vinegar*
     Salt
     Freshly ground black pepper

Wash, dry and thoroughly chill lettuce leaves before placing on cold salad plate. Arrange sliced tomatoes on lettuce leaves and sprinkle with garlic.

Blend oil, vinegar, salt and pepper to taste until salt is dissolved, and pour lightly over tomatoes.

STRING BEAN SALAD

READY TRAY   Serves 4

1   *pound string beans, cut in half, cooked and cooled*
4   *tablespoons olive oil*
2   *tablespoons wine vinegar*
1   *onion, thinly sliced*
1   *clove garlic, finely chopped*
1   *teaspoon fresh parsley, finely chopped*
     Salt and pepper
     Lettuce leaves
1   *hard-cooked egg, chopped*
     Grated Parmesan cheese

Place cooked beans in a salad bowl. Combine the oil, vinegar, onion, garlic, parsley, and salt and pepper to

32

taste. Pour over the beans and mix lightly. Cover and chill thoroughly in refrigerator.

Serve on crisp lettuce leaves on individual salad plates, and sprinkle lightly with chopped egg and cheese before serving.

This is also excellent as an antipasto course.

CHEF SALAD, ITALIAN STYLE

READY TRAY   Serves 4 to 6

2   large cloves garlic
½   teaspoon onion salt
1   tablespoon red wine vinegar
4   tablespoons olive oil
½   teaspoon freshly ground black pepper
½   teaspoon dry mustard
¼   pound salami, thinly sliced and julienned
¼   pound provolone cheese, thinly sliced and julienned
1   cup chicory, torn in bite-size pieces
1   cup escarole, torn in bite-size pieces
1   cup finocchio (fennel), thinly sliced
1   cup Belgian endive, cut in 1-inch pieces
1   cup watercress
1   tablespoon salted capers
¼   cup chopped black olives
2   tablespoons grated Parmesan cheese

Rub wooden salad bowl well with garlic, discard cloves. Dissolve onion salt thoroughly in vinegar in salad bowl. Slowly add oil, pepper and mustard, stirring well. Add salami, cheese, greens and remaining ingredients. Toss lightly. More vinegar or oil may be added to taste.

Serve on cold salad plates.

33

Sauces for Pasta

The tomato did not originate in Italy. It is native to Central and South America, and Cortes is credited with introducing it into Spain, to be eaten as a fruit. The cultivation of the tomato spread from Spain across the Pyrenees into France and over the Alps into Italy, but when its novelty as a fruit diminished, southern Italy, whose hot climate provided perfect ripening conditions, was the only place in Europe where it continued to be cultivated. The housewives of the region began experimenting with it in preparing their daily meals, and *salsa di pomodoro* is the happy result.

Some basic and distinctive recipes follow, with simple step-by-step instructions. Where water is called for, try substituting clam juice for a different flavor. But if clam juice is added, make only enough sauce for immediate use because it will not keep.

Every city and hamlet in Italy claims its sauce is the authentic and best one. Certainly the variations are many, and each sauce has its merits. Let your own creativeness and imagination inspire you in preparing your special sauce.

BASIC TOMATO SAUCE

READY TRAY   Makes 2 cups

1   *No. 2½ can solid-pack tomatoes*
1   *large onion, finely chopped*
2   *large cloves garlic, finely chopped*
2   *tablespoons olive oil*
4   *tablespoons butter*
1   *bay leaf*
1   *teaspoon oregano*
    Salt and pepper

In a large heavy saucepan quickly sauté onion and garlic in oil and butter, until wilted. Add tomato pulp (which has been pressed through a strainer) and remaining ingredients, and blend thoroughly. Simmer uncovered over low heat until the sauce is thickened, approximately one hour. Stir from time to time and add a small quantity of water if sauce is thickening too rapidly.

34

Fresh tomatoes can be substituted. Peel and chop them finely, using pulp only and adding hot broth or water for necessary liquid.

If tomato puree is used, simmer slowly for 45 minutes, adding a little hot broth or water to maintain thick consistency, stirring often. Tomato paste should first be diluted to thickness of a tomato puree.

Your taste buds will tell you when the desired sweetness of the tomato sauce has been achieved.

TOMATO SAUCE WITH SALT PORK

READY TRAY   Makes 2 cups

½   pound salt pork, cut in 1-inch pieces
1   large onion, finely chopped
2   cloves garlic, finely chopped
1   tablespoon parsley, finely chopped
1   No. 2½ can solid-pack tomatoes
1   bay leaf
    Pinch of spice, your choice
    Salt and pepper

Sauté salt pork, onion, garlic and parsley until golden brown.

Add the strained tomato pulp and juice to the sautéed pork and onion. Add bay leaf, spice, and salt and pepper to taste. Simmer gently over low heat, adding liquid as necessary, for approximately 1 hour. Don't forget to stir from time to time.

GARLIC AND OIL SAUCE

READY TRAY

5   cloves garlic, finely chopped
4   tablespoons olive oil
4   tablespoons grated Parmesan cheese
    Pepper

Place garlic with oil in the kettle in which pasta was cooked, over low heat. As soon as garlic is golden brown, add the cooked pasta and remove from heat. Stir gently until oil is absorbed.

Season to taste with pepper, sprinkle with cheese and mix lightly. Cheese may be added to individual taste.

This is good with spaghetti or spaghettini and is a change from the usual tomato sauce.

MARINARA SAUCE

READY TRAY   Makes 2 cups

3   cloves garlic, finely chopped
2   teaspoons basil, finely chopped
2   tablespoons parsley, finely chopped
4   tablespoons olive oil
6   ripe tomatoes, peeled, seeded and finely chopped
                    or
1   No. 2½ can solid-pack tomatoes, diced
    Salt and pepper

Sauté garlic, basil and parsley in oil until golden brown.

Add tomatoes and cook slowly, stirring occasionally, until thick. Add a little hot broth or water as needed.

Season to taste with salt and pepper.

TOMATO SAUCE WITH SPARERIBS

READY TRAY   Makes 2 cups

1   No. 2 can peeled Italian-style tomatoes
                    or
2   pounds homegrown ripe tomatoes
½   can tomato paste (scant)
½   pound spareribs
    Olive oil
    Sprigs of parsley with stems
1   teaspoon sugar
    Salt

Combine tomatoes and paste and let simmer gently for 20 minutes.

In another saucepan, sauté spareribs in sufficient oil to brown on all sides. When browned, remove meat and add to tomato sauce. Then strain oil into the sauce.

Add parsley leaves with stems, sugar and salt. Simmer to desired thickness, stirring from time to time and add-

36

ing water if sauce becomes thick too soon. Allow 1 hour cooking time.

Pork steak or boneless stewing veal, cut up in 1½-inch pieces, can be substituted for spareribs.

ANCHOVY SAUCE

READY TRAY   Makes 2 cups

8   *tablespoons olive oil*
20 *anchovy fillets, coarsely chopped*
    Black pepper
2   *cups prepared tomato sauce*
4   *tablespoons butter*

Place oil in saucepan over low heat. Add anchovies and mash lightly. Season to taste with pepper.
Add tomato sauce and butter and heat thoroughly. This is a good sauce with spaghetti.

PAPA'S PESTO

READY TRAY

4   *cloves garlic, peeled*
½   *cup fresh basil leaves*
4   *tablespoons olive oil*
4   *tablespoons grated Parmesan cheese*

Although it is preferable to use a mortar and pestle in preparing this sauce, an electric blender may be used. Place garlic, basil and oil into blender and blend until a smooth paste is formed. Add cheese and blend thoroughly.
If mortar is available, crush garlic first with the pestle until fine. Add basil leaves and crush until fine and smooth. Add oil and cheese and blend thoroughly.
This is excellent served over tagliarini, adding a little of the pesto at a time and tossing lightly until sauce is used up.

A variation that is highly recommended is the addition of ¼ cup of pine nuts, crushed and blended.

37

MUSHROOM SAUCE

Makes 3 cups

1   onion, finely chopped
⅓   cup olive oil
1   pound fresh mushrooms, sliced (canned may be substituted)
1   large clove garlic, finely chopped
2   cups canned tomatoes, chopped
1   bay leaf
1   teaspoon parsley, finely chopped
¼   teaspoon oregano
     Salt and pepper

      Sauté onion in oil until wilted. Add mushrooms and garlic, brown lightly. Add tomatoes with juice, bring to a quick boil over high heat. Lower heat, add bay leaf, parsley, oregano, salt and pepper to taste. Simmer gently until reduced and thickened.

TOMATO SAUCE WITH CHICKEN LIVERS

READY TRAY   Makes 2 cups

1   No. 2½ can solid-pack tomatoes
4   tablespoons butter
6   tablespoons olive oil
2   tablespoons parsley, finely chopped
2   tablespoons fresh sweet basil, finely chopped
     Salt and pepper
½   pound chicken livers, cut in small pieces
1   bunch fresh green onions, finely chopped
2   cloves garlic, finely chopped
¼   cup white table wine

      Melt butter with 2 tablespoons oil in a large saucepan. Add strained tomato pulp and juice, parsley, basil, and season to taste with salt and pepper. Blend thoroughly and simmer gently over low heat, adding liquid if needed from time to time. Sauce will be reduced and thickened in approximately 1 hour.
      Lightly sauté chicken livers, onions and garlic in 4 tablespoons oil until golden brown. Add wine, simmer for 5 minutes, then add to tomato sauce and blend thoroughly.

BUTTER SAUCE

Makes ¼ cup

¼ *pound butter*
2 *teaspoons parsley, finely chopped*
   Freshly ground black pepper
   Grated Parmesan or Romano cheese

> Melt butter in saucepan over medium heat. Add parsley and pepper to taste.
> Serve over cooked spaghetti, linguini or your favorite pasta, well drained. Toss lightly and sprinkle generously with grated cheese.

MEAT SAUCE

READY TRAY   Makes 4 cups

½ *pound fine ground round steak*
¼ *pound fine ground veal*
¼ *pound fine ground pork*
⅛ *pound fine ground ham*
3 *tablespoons olive oil*
2 *tablespoons butter*
1 *large onion, finely chopped*
1 *large clove garlic, finely chopped*
2 *stalks celery with leaves, finely chopped*
1 *carrot, grated*
1 *tablespoon parsley, finely chopped*
1 *bay leaf*
½ *teaspoon fennel seeds*
½ *teaspoon oregano*
½ *teaspoon allspice*
⅛ *teaspoon nutmeg*
1 *tablespoon sugar*
   Salt and pepper
2 *tablespoons flour*
2 *cups canned tomatoes, drained and chopped*
1½ *cups tomato juice from canned tomatoes; add water or beef or chicken broth to make enough liquid*
2 *tablespoons tomato paste, diluted with equal part water*
½ *cup dry white wine*
¼ *pound fresh mushrooms, sliced thin*

39

In a large saucepan thoroughly brown meats in oil and butter, breaking up meat with a fork.

Add onion, garlic, celery, carrots, parsley, bay leaf, spices, sugar, salt and pepper to taste, and flour. Blend with meats and sauté quickly over high heat until vegetables are wilted, approximately 5 minutes.

Reduce heat, stir in tomatoes, juice, diluted tomato paste and wine. Cover and simmer about 1½ hours until reduced to thick sauce, stirring occasionally and adding liquid as necessary.

Add mushrooms and simmer until tender. Serve with spaghetti, macaroni or the heavier pasta. When adding sauce to pasta, fold sauce in gently a little at a time, putting extra sauce over the top and sprinkling with grated cheese and chopped parsley.

If all of the sauce is not used, it may be frozen and kept for future use. Be sure that it is completely cooled at room temperature before freezing.

CLAM SAUCE

READY TRAY   Makes 2 cups

1   large clove garlic, finely chopped
4   tablespoons olive oil
¼   cup water
2   teaspoons parsley, finely chopped
½   teaspoon salt
½   teaspoon oregano leaves
¼   teaspoon freshly ground black pepper
1   cup Little Neck clams and juice, preferably
     fresh clams when available
2   tablespoons butter
2   tablespoons flour
½   teaspoon monosodium glutamate
1   cup milk

Sauté garlic in oil until golden brown. Add water, parsley, salt, oregano and pepper. Mix gently. Add clams and juice; cover and simmer gently until clams are heated thoroughly.

Melt butter in saucepan over low heat and blend in flour and monosodium glutamate until smooth. Remove from heat, add milk slowly, blending thoroughly. Return

40

to heat and bring to quick boil, stirring constantly. Cook 5 minutes.

Add clams to white sauce and stir gently before serving over linguini or tagliarini.

RED CLAM SAUCE

Makes 2 cups

1   *large clove garlic, finely chopped*
4   *tablespoons olive oil*
2   *cups canned tomatoes, finely chopped*
2   *teaspoons parsley, finely chopped*
½   *teaspoon salt*
½   *teaspoon oregano leaves*
¼   *teaspoon freshly ground black pepper*
1   *cup Little Neck clams and juice, preferably fresh clams when available*

Sauté garlic in oil until golden brown. Add tomatoes, parsley, salt, oregano and pepper. Mix gently and simmer 30 minutes. Add clams and juice, cover and continue to simmer slowly until clams are heated thoroughly.

Serve over linguini or tagliarini.

Pasta - Gnocchi - Polenta

Picture an Italian grandmother, usually with a grandchild or two under foot, in her old-fashioned kitchen as she rolls out dough, kneads, cuts and shapes it, effortlessly and quickly—a procedure done so many times that her hands move too fast to see how she twirls and twists the dough into those intriguing shapes. Then savor the freshly made pasta in a freshly cooked sauce, whose tantalizing fragrance filled the kitchen as it simmered on the stove. Nothing will ever taste as good again!

Making your own pasta takes time and know-how. Still, there are machines available to help you save time in cutting and shaping the dough, and with practice comes the know-how.

Spaghetti derives its name from *spago*, which means a thick twine. *Macaroni*, according to legend, owes its name to a man who invented a machine to make a new kind of tubular pasta. A simple identification of the various types of pasta follows:

1. Ropes and strings: spaghetti, spaghettini and vermicelli (fine, finer and finest).
2. Tubular forms: macaroni, mostaccioli, ditalini, mezzani, rigatoni, ziti.
3. Flat ribbons: noodles, tagliarini, linguini, fettuccine (the narrowest) to lasagne (the widest).
4. Envelopes or small pillows, the filled pastas: ravioli (various-sized small squares), tortellini (half-moons), cappelletti (little hats), manicotti (little muffs) and cannelloni (big pipes).
5. Fancy shapes: pastina (very small in various shapes, mainly used in soups), shells, wagon wheels, butterflies and lemon slices.

BASIC NOODLE DOUGH

READY TRAY   Serves 4

4   cups flour
½   teaspoon salt
4   eggs
4   tablespoons cold water
    Olive oil

Sift flour and salt into a large bowl. Make a well in center of flour and add eggs, one at a time, mixing lightly after each addition. Add water and a few drops of oil, adding more water and oil to form a firm dough. Mix thoroughly until it forms a ball.

Place ball of dough on lightly floured board and using heels of your hands, gently push dough away from you. Give it a quarter turn; repeat process, with rhythm, until dough is smooth and elastic—about 10 minutes—adding as little flour as possible. Always turn dough in the same direction. The more the dough is kneaded, the better.

Divide kneaded dough in two parts and form into balls. Cover and let rest 10 to 15 minutes before proceeding.

Roll out dough with a rolling pin on lightly floured board until very thin or until you can see the shape of your hand through the dough. Try to roll it out into a rectangular shape. Beginning with the narrow end, gently fold over about 2 inches of dough and continue to fold over, like a jelly roll, until final width is about 3 inches in diameter. Dough must be dry enough so that the layers do not stick together, when rolled.

Beginning at the narrow edge, with a sharp knife cut dough into strips ⅛ inch wide for noodles, and wider for other varieties of pasta. Unroll strips carefully and arrange on a lightly floured cloth or waxed paper so that they are lying flat. Let the noodles dry for 1 to 2 hours before cooking.

A variety of forms, sizes and shapes may be made from this basic dough.

General Cooking Directions

In a large kettle, bring 5 quarts of water to a rapid rolling boil for 1 pound of pasta. Add 1 tablespoon of salt and when water comes to a hard boil again, put in the pasta. Never break it, if it is in longer lengths. Just hold the pasta in your hand, place ends in bottom of kettle and push the spaghetti or noodles down gently until submerged in the boiling water. A little oil or butter added to the boiling water will keep the pasta from sticking together. Stir from time to time with a long-handled spoon.

Boil pasta uncovered to al dente stage, that is, when it is firm to the bite. Test it from time to time to be sure not to overcook it. The length of time required will vary with the thickness of the pasta, the variety, whether it is homemade, etc.

Drain pasta thoroughly in a colander and transfer immediately to large heated serving dish. When adding sauce, it is a good idea to ladle a small amount over the pasta and toss it lightly so that the pasta is coated before the remainder of the sauce is poured over it. Sprinkle with grated Parmesan cheese, preferably freshly ground for better flavor, and a little fresh chopped parsley for color, if desired.

CANNELLONI

READY TRAY   Serves 6

1   recipe basic noodle dough
1   recipe filling, your choice
½   cup tomato sauce
    Grated Parmesan cheese

Roll dough out into a very thin sheet, and sprinkle with flour. Cut into rectangles 3 by 4 inches. Dry for 1 hour. Cook in boiling salted water 5 minutes. Drain well.

Spread filling on cooked rectangles and roll up like a jelly roll.

Butter a deep casserole and spread ¼ cup tomato sauce over the bottom. Arrange cannelloni on it, cover with remaining tomato sauce, sprinkle with ¼ cup grated cheese. Bake uncovered in 450° oven 10 to 15 minutes.

RAVIOLI
(FILLED SQUARES)

READY TRAY   Serves 6

1   recipe basic noodle dough
1   recipe filling, your choice

Prepare basic noodle dough. Divide dough into 4 parts and lightly roll out each part to ⅛-inch thickness in a rectangular shape. If ravioli pin is used, spread the filling over half of the dough. Completely cover with other half of dough. Place ravioli pin on dough, and rolling it away from you slowly, with a gentle force, press dough into miniature filled squares. With a pastry cutter, cut through to separate squares.

If ravioli pin is not available, cut dough into circles with a biscuit cutter or medium-size glass. Place rounded teaspoon of filling on half of each circle, fold other half over and press edges together with tines of a fork. If edges are a little dry, dampen with a little water before pressing tines of fork into the dough.

Or, using a pastry cutter, the dough may be cut lengthwise into strips 4 inches wide. Place rounded teaspoon of filling in center of strip, 3 inches apart, along half of the strip. Fold each strip over in half lengthwise, covering the mounds of filling. To seal, press edges together with tines of fork and press gently between mounds to form rectangles about 2 inches long. Cut apart with pastry cutter, pressing edges with tines of fork. Dry on lightly floured board for an hour or longer before cooking.

To cook, bring 5 quarts of water to rapid, rolling boil. Add 1 tablespoon salt and bring again to vigorous boil. Add a few ravioli at a time to the boiling water and cook uncovered approximately 15 to 20 minutes, or until tender. A little oil added to the boiling water will give the ravioli a glossy appearance, when cooked.

When the ravioli rise to the top of the kettle, this does not necessarily mean that they are thoroughly cooked. Be sure to test before removing from water. Stir gently from the bottom of the kettle with a long-handled wooden spoon to prevent sticking. Drain well before adding sauce.

Ravioli may be frozen for future use by placing them on a lightly floured piece of cardboard and covering with saran wrap, before placing in freezer. Thaw thoroughly before cooking.

TORTELLINI

(HALF MOONS)

READY TRAY   Serves 6

1   recipe basic noodle dough
1   recipe filling, your choice

Prepare basic noodle dough and cut with biscuit cutter or medium-size glass into small circles. Fill half of each circle with filling and press edges together with tines of a fork to seal.

Dry for an hour or longer on lightly floured board and cook in the same way as ravioli.

CAPPELLETTI

(LITTLE HATS)   Serves 6

These are prepared in the same manner as tortellini. Then take the filled half-moon shapes, bring the two points together and press until edges stick together, forming the shape of little Swiss hats.

CHICKEN FILLING

READY TRAY

1   pair lamb or veal brains
2   pairs sweetbreads
2   tablespoons butter
¼   pound chicken livers, cut in small pieces
1   large chicken breast, boned and cut in small pieces
⅓   cup chicken or beef broth
1   thin slice prosciutto, finely chopped
1   cup cooked spinach or Swiss chard, drained and chopped
2   egg yolks
2   tablespoons grated Parmesan cheese
½   teaspoon ground cloves
½   teaspoon salt
     Breadcrumbs

Parboil brains and sweetbreads. Remove thin outer skins. Wash thoroughly, dry and cut in small pieces.

Place butter in frying pan, add brains, sweetbreads, chicken livers and chicken breast. Sauté gently over low heat until golden brown. Add broth, cover and cook until tender, adding a little more liquid as needed. Drain well, add prosciutto and put through meat grinder several times, using fine blade.

Place in a bowl and add spinach, egg yolks, cheese, cloves, salt and a few breadcrumbs to bind. Mix thoroughly.

46

RICOTTA CHEESE FILLING

READY TRAY

2   *eggs, lightly beaten*
1   *cup cooked Swiss chard, finely chopped*
1   *pound ricotta, drained*
½   *cup grated Parmesan cheese*
¼   *teaspoon ground cloves*
    Pinch of cinnamon
    Salt
    Fine breadcrumbs

To beaten eggs, add Swiss chard, ricotta, grated cheese, cloves, cinnamon, salt to taste and a few breadcrumbs. Blend thoroughly until smooth.

Add a few more breadcrumbs if the mixture is too soft and watery. It should be slightly firm when placed on the dough.

SPINACH FILLING

READY TRAY

1   *cup cooked spinach or Swiss chard, finely chopped*
2   *tablespoons prosciutto, finely chopped*
1   *slice mortadella, finely chopped*
⅛   *pound beef marrow, finely chopped*
4   *tablespoons grated Parmesan cheese*
1   *egg, lightly beaten*
    Pinch cinnamon
    Salt and pepper to taste
¼   *cup breadcrumbs*

Using a large bowl, combine all ingredients and blend thoroughly until smooth. Add another egg yolk or more breadcrumbs, if needed, to maintain a firm texture.

FETTUCCINE ALFREDO

The king of noodles is fettuccine. Alfredo of Rome built an international reputation for himself simply by making them fresh every day, boiling them 8 or 9 minutes, and then putting them in a chafing dish to which he added great quantities of fresh sweet butter, lots of grated Parmesan cheese and a little rich cream, tossing them all the while with a wooden fork and spoon. Today only the implements are different. A golden fork and spoon are used and are inscribed: "To Alfredo, King of the Noodles—Mary Pickford, Douglas Fairbanks, July, 1927."

This is an excellent dish for the host to display his artistry and showmanship at the dinner table.

READY TRAY   Serves 4 to 6

1   *pound fettuccine (flat narrow noodles)*
1   *tablespoon olive oil*
¼   *pound sweet butter*
¾   *cup grated Parmesan cheese*
½   *cup rich, fresh sweet cream*
1   *egg, lightly beaten*
     Salt and freshly ground black pepper

Cook noodles until tender, 8 to 10 minutes, in salted boiling water with 1 tablespoon oil added to prevent sticking. Drain thoroughly in colander.

Melt butter in chafing dish, or in kettle over medium heat. Add cheese, cream, beaten egg gradually and blend until slightly thickened. Add noodles, salt and freshly ground black pepper to taste and toss lightly until noodles are coated evenly with sauce. Serve on hot plates and garnish with additional cheese.

FETTUCCINE ALMONDINE

READY TRAY   Serves 4 to 6

1   *pound thin egg noodles, commercial or homemade*
4   *tablespoons butter*
1   *cup grated Parmesan cheese*
¾   *cup toasted slivered almonds*
½   *cup heavy cream*
2   *tablespoons sliced green onions*
     Salt and pepper

Cook noodles in salted boiling water until tender, and drain thoroughly.

Melt butter over low heat, add noodles and stir care-

48

fully until well coated. Add cheese, almonds, cream, onions, salt and pepper to taste. Toss lightly until thoroughly blended and serve immediately.

GREEN NOODLES

READY TRAY   Serves 4 to 6

1   *recipe basic noodle dough*
½   *pound finely chopped cooked spinach*
¾   *cup grated Parmesan cheese*
¼   *pound sweet butter*

> To make green noodles, add ½ pound finely chopped cooked spinach (use blender to prepare spinach) to the basic dough, and proceed in same manner.
> Cook noodles in boiling water with salt until tender. Drain thoroughly.
> Place one-third of the noodles into a casserole, top with one-third of cheese and one-third of butter, cut in small pieces. Repeat layers ending with cheese and butter.
> Bake in 350° oven for 15 to 20 minutes, until the cheese is melted.

STUFFED LASAGNE

READY TRAY   Serves 6 to 8

½   *pound lean veal ground with*
½   *pound lean pork*
1   *clove garlic, finely chopped*
⅓   *cup parsley, finely chopped*
2   *tablespoons grated Parmesan cheese*
1   *egg, lightly beaten*
    Salt and pepper
    Fine breadcrumbs
    Olive oil
1   *pound lasagne (broad noodles)*
2   *cups prepared basic tomato sauce*
½   *pound mozzarella cheese, sliced thin*

49

Mix ground meat thoroughly with garlic. Add parsley, grated cheese, egg, salt and pepper to taste and enough breadcrumbs so mixture will be firm. Shape into ½-inch balls. Brown lightly in oil on all sides, one layer at a time.

Cook lasagne in 5 quarts rapidly boiling salted water until tender, about 20 minutes. Remove from heat and add 2 cups cold water to kettle to cool the lasagne, and also to keep from sticking together. Drain thoroughly.

Pour enough tomato sauce to thinly cover bottom of casserole, 2 inches deep and 12 inches square. Place a layer of lasagne over the sauce, then a layer of meatballs 2 inches apart, and ladle a little sauce evenly over the top. Add another layer of lasagne, a layer of mozzarella cheese slices placed close together and cover lightly with tomato sauce.

Continue alternating layers of lasagne, meatballs and sauce and lasagne, cheese and sauce, until all ingredients are used. Sprinkle ½ cup grated cheese over the top layer, cover casserole and bake in 350° oven 20 minutes. Remove cover and let top brown lightly 5 to 7 minutes.

To serve, cut in 2-inch squares. Serve with additional sauce, if desired.

BAKED LASAGNE

READY TRAY   Serves 6 to 8

1   pound lasagne
1   pound ricotta
1   pint milk
2   eggs, lightly beaten
1   tablespoon parsley, finely chopped
    Salt
¼   teaspoon cinnamon
½   pound scamozza cheese, or, if not available, mozzarella cheese
    Olive oil
1   pound ground lean beef
3   cups tomato sauce
    Grated Parmesan cheese

Cook lasagne in large quantity of rapidly boiling salted water to al dente stage. Drain and set aside, handling strips carefully to keep them whole.

Cream ricotta with milk (if ricotta is very liquid, less

50

milk should be used). Add beaten eggs, parsley, salt and cinnamon. Dice scamozza or mozzarella cheese into ½-inch cubes, and add to ricotta mixture.

Sauté ground beef in oil until browned, and add two or three tablespoons of tomato sauce to it to moisten.

Oil a rectangular baking dish and spoon some of the ricotta mixture over bottom of dish. Start with a layer of lasagne, cover with ricotta mixture and ground meat, and sprinkle with grated cheese. Continue with layers of lasagne and filling, ending with lasagne strips.

Cover the baking dish with waxed paper cut to fit, oiled on the outside, and bake in 350° oven for 1 hour.

To serve, cut into individual portions and put a serving of tomato sauce, to the taste of the individual, over each portion. Fill a gravy boat with the remaining sauce, and pass as desired.

This is an excellent dish for a buffet because the delicate blend of flavors improves with standing. The sauce should, of course, be served thoroughly heated.

MANICOTTI WITH RICOTTA FILLING
(CREPE STYLE)

READY TRAY   Serves 4

3	medium-size eggs
1	cup flour, sifted
1½	cup milk
1	tablespoon olive oil
	Dash of salt
1	pound creamy ricotta cheese
¼	cup parsley, finely chopped
1	egg, beaten
¼	cup grated Parmesan cheese
2	cups prepared tomato sauce

These manicotti are small crepes or pancakes, and not made from a rolled-out dough. To make the batter, beat eggs, which should be at room temperature, and add flour gradually. Add milk, olive oil and salt, stirring with a fork to make a smooth batter. Don't overbeat.

Heat an iron griddle or a large skillet or a small heavy pan thoroughly, and if it is well seasoned or has a Teflon surface, no oil is needed. Place a heaping table-

51

spoon of batter on the griddle or pan, and spread and shape it as you go, working rapidly. It only takes a minute or two for the pancake to cook. The finished crepe is about 5 inches in diameter, and on a large griddle or skillet, several can be made at one time. The pancakes can be larger if you choose, but the small ones make a more attractive dish.

When the bottom of the crepe is lightly browned and it can be lifted up easily with a spatula, it is cooked. Do not turn it, but transfer crepe, being careful not to break it, to a flat dish. As you stack the crepes, the cooked side goes on the unbrowned side—but don't worry, they won't stick together. This part can be done several days in advance. You will get about 24 to 28 crepes from this amount of batter. Just refrigerate them, don't freeze, covered with waxed paper.

The filling should be prepared on the day you plan to serve the manicotti. In a mixing bowl, beat ricotta with a spoon, add parsley, salt and Parmesan cheese. Then add beaten egg and blend thoroughly.

To fill, place a generous tablespoon of filling in the middle of the crepe on the uncooked side. Roll it up like a small jelly roll, and place in the baking dish, seam side down. (Spoon a thin layer of tomato sauce over the bottom of the baking dish first.) This can be done in the morning and the manicotti refrigerated until you are ready to put them in the oven. Then cover them with a light layer of sauce and bake in a preheated 350° oven until bubbling hot, about 20 minutes. Serve with rest of sauce, which should be very hot.

This is a good buffet-party dish as it can wait to be eaten, it is easily served and the flavor is a delicate light one which goes well with other foods.

POTATO GNOCCHI

READY TRAY   Serves 4

2   potatoes, peeled
    Flour
    Tomato sauce or meat sauce, your choice
    Grated Parmesan cheese

Cook potatoes in salted water until tender. Drain, mash and place on floured mixing board. Knead in a little flour at a time thoroughly, adding flour as needed to form a firm dough—approximately one cup of flour to one potato. A beaten egg yolk may be added, if desired. Set aside for 15 minutes.

On a lightly floured board, roll the dough into narrow strips, about 12 inches long by ⅜ inches thick. Cut the strips into ½-inch pieces, and sprinkle them lightly with flour. Dry for an hour or more before cooking.

If a more elaborate gnocchi is desired, continue as follows: Take a grater and lightly flour the side with the smallest holes, facing upward. Place one of the cut pieces of dough on the grater, then press and push your thumb with a flourish over the dough, which will take the shape of a small shell rolled over on itself. A little practice will enable you to make them of a uniform thickness. Open them flat, place on a well-floured board and dry out before cooking.

Cook in a large amount of salted water for 20 to 30 minutes, depending upon thickness. Drain and add sauce, mix lightly and sprinkle with cheese. This is an excellent way to use leftover mashed potatoes.

GNOCCHI WITH BREAST OF CHICKEN

READY TRAY   Serves 4 to 6

1   *pound raw potatoes, peeled*
2   *breasts of chicken*
2   *tablespoons grated Parmesan cheese*
2   *egg yolks*
¼   *cup flour*
   Dash of nutmeg, freshly grated if possible
   Salt
1   *cup tomato sauce*
   Grated Parmesan cheese
   Freshly ground black pepper
2   *tablespoons parsley, finely chopped*

Boil potatoes until tender and force through a sieve into a large bowl. Boil chicken breasts until tender. Bone and put through fine grinder.

Add chicken to potatoes with the grated cheese, egg yolks, flour, nutmeg and salt to taste. Mix thoroughly and turn out on floured mixing board. Knead gently to the consistency of a pie dough. Add more flour or water, if needed. Cover with a clean cloth and let rest for 15 minutes, then knead again for a few minutes.

Cut dough into pieces the size of an egg. Roll these out in strips of ⅜-inch thickness. Cut the strips into ½-inch pieces and sprinkle lightly with flour. Make a firm indentation with your thumb in each gnocchi so that they will have a uniform thickness.

Cover bottom of 2-quart casserole with a little of the tomato sauce. Place layer of gnocchi in the casserole, sprinkle with grated cheese, season to taste with pepper. Repeat until all ingredients are used. Cover top layer with rest of tomato sauce and sprinkle with parsley.

Cover and place in 350° oven. Bake 30 minutes, or until gnocchi are tender.

SPAGHETTI WITH MEATBALLS

READY TRAY   Serves 6 to 8

½	pound bread, trimmed and cut into ½-inch cubes
	Beef or chicken broth
½	pound lean beef finely ground with
½	pound lean veal and
½	pound lean pork
3	egg yolks, beaten very lightly
6	tablespoons grated Parmesan cheese
1	small bunch parsley, finely chopped
1	clove garlic, finely chopped
1	teaspoon allspice
	Salt and pepper
	Oil
2	cups prepared tomato sauce
1½	pounds spaghetti
	Grated Parmesan cheese

Place bread in saucepan over low heat; add broth a tablespoonful at a time and blend until smooth but not too soft. Remove from heat and cool thoroughly.

Place moistened, cooled bread in a large bowl and add meat, egg yolks, cheese, parsley, garlic, allspice, and salt and pepper to taste. Mix thoroughly and shape into small balls 1-inch in diameter, rolling meat between palms of your hands. Fry in oil, one layer at a time, until lightly browned on all sides. Set aside and keep warm. Drop browned meatballs in thoroughly heated tomato sauce and cook over low heat until done.

Boil spaghetti in 5 quarts rapidly boiling salted water until tender. Drain and serve on individual dinner plates, with the meatballs and sauce served in a separate bowl. Serve grated cheese separately.

The sauce and meatballs may be prepared as much as a day in advance and refrigerated.

POLENTA

READY TRAY   Serves 4

1   cup yellow cornmeal
3   cups water
1   teaspoon salt
2   tablespoons olive oil

Bring salted water with oil to rapid boil and slowly pour in cornmeal, stirring constantly with a wire whisk or wooden spoon to prevent lumps from forming. Reduce heat, stirring slowly; cook until polenta is well thickened.

If cooked to a firm stage, the polenta may be turned out on a slab and cut into pieces and served in place of bread. When cooked to a softer consistency, similar to mashed potatoes, it is served with a sauce and sprinkled with grated cheese.

Or the polenta may be baked, alternating layers of polenta, sauce and cheese.

Risottos

There are numerous ways to prepare rice, which is a staple of northern Italian cooking as pasta is a staple of southern Italian. The risotto is the most common and popular way, and it can be prepared by two methods. The ingredients and cooking time are the same for both.

One method is to cook the entire recipe over direct heat on top of the stove, stirring steadily, adding liquid gradually, and cooking until the rice and ingredients are tender. This takes approximately 30 to 40 minutes. It is excellent prepared in this way, but it demands constant attention.

The second method is to start the risotto over direct heat, but to complete its cooking in the oven. This has the advantage of allowing more time for preparing other dishes for the meal which is being readied.

The recipes in this section use the second or "oven" method of preparation.

RISOTTO MILANESE

READY TRAY   Serves 4 to 6

1   *onion, finely chopped*
3   *tablespoons butter*
1   *cup rice*
3   *cups beef or chicken broth, heated thoroughly*
     Salt and pepper
     Pinch of saffron
4   *tablespoons grated Parmesan cheese*

Sauté onion lightly in butter. Add rice and stir until butter is absorbed. Add hot broth, salt and pepper to taste, and saffron and bring to a boil, stirring constantly.

Pour into a 2-quart casserole and bake uncovered in 350° oven, approximately 30 to 40 minutes, until rice is tender and liquid is absorbed.

Dot top with butter and sprinkle with cheese before serving.

For added flavor, capers and mushrooms can be added before placing the casserole in oven.

56

ANCHOVY RISOTTO

Serves 4 to 6

4   tablespoons olive oil
8   anchovy fillets
6   dried mushrooms, soaked, drained and finely chopped
1   onion, finely chopped
8   tablespoons butter
1   cup rice
3   cups hot broth or water
    Pepper
    Pinch ground cloves
    Pinch saffron powder
½   cup grated Parmesan cheese

Heat oil in small saucepan. Add anchovies and mash thoroughly with a fork. Do not let oil reach frying temperature. Add mushrooms and set aside.

Sauté onion in butter until wilted. Add rice and stir until butter is absorbed. Add broth or water, pepper to taste. (Salt is not needed because the anchovies are salty.) Stir thoroughly and slowly bring to a boil.

Pour into a casserole, bake uncovered in 350° oven for 15 minutes. Add anchovies with mushrooms, cloves, saffron, cheese; blend thoroughly. Return to oven and bake 15 to 20 minutes longer.

CACCIATORE RISOTTO
(HUNTER STYLE)

Serves 4 to 6

1   broiler chicken, 1½ to 2 pounds, cut in bite-size pieces
4   tablespoons butter
2   slices bacon, finely chopped
2   cloves garlic, finely chopped
6   tablespoons tomato sauce
3   cups broth
1   tablespoon parsley, finely chopped
1   cup rice
    Salt and pepper
4   tablespoons grated Parmesan cheese

Sauté chicken in butter and bacon until well browned. Add garlic and when it is golden brown, add tomato sauce, broth, parsley, rice, salt and pepper to taste, and bring to a slow boil, stirring constantly.

Pour into a large casserole and bake uncovered in 350° oven approximately 30 minutes, until rice is tender and liquid is absorbed.

Add cheese, blend and serve.

RISOTTO WITH TOMATOES

READY TRAY   Serves 4 to 6

8	tablespoons butter
1	cup rice
1½	cups prepared basic tomato sauce
1½	cups hot broth, beef or chicken
	Salt and pepper
4	tablespoons grated Parmesan cheese

Melt butter in large saucepan over direct heat. Add rice and stir until butter is absorbed.

Blend tomato sauce with hot broth and add to rice. Salt and pepper to taste, and bring to boil, stirring constantly.

Pour into a large casserole and bake uncovered in 350° oven for approximately 30 minutes, until liquid is absorbed. Add a little broth and bake a few minutes longer if it appears to be overdry.

Sprinkle with cheese before serving.

CHICKEN LIVERS RISOTTO

READY TRAY   Serves 4 to 6

1	onion, finely chopped
¼	pound button mushrooms, cut in ½-inch pieces
½	pound chicken livers, cut in ½-inch pieces
8	tablespoons butter
1	cup rice
3	cups chicken broth
	Salt and pepper
	Pinch saffron powder
4	tablespoons grated Parmesan cheese

Sauté onion, mushrooms and chicken livers in butter until golden brown.

Add rice, stir until butter is absorbed. Add broth and bring to a slow boil, stirring constantly. Add salt and pepper to taste and saffron.

Pour into large casserole, bake uncovered in 350° oven for 30 minutes, until liquid is absorbed.

Add cheese, stir lightly and serve hot.

SQUAB RISOTTO

READY TRAY   Serves 4

2 squabs, split in halves
4 tablespoons butter
2 slices bacon, finely chopped
2 cloves garlic, finely chopped
6 tablespoons tomato sauce
3 cups broth
1 tablespoon parsley, finely chopped
1 cup rice
   Salt and pepper
4 tablespoons grated Parmesan cheese

Sauté squabs in butter and bacon until well browned. Add garlic and when golden brown, add tomato sauce, broth, parsley, rice, salt and pepper to taste, and bring to a boil, stirring gently.

Pour into a large casserole and bake uncovered in 350° oven 30 minutes or until all ingredients are tender.

Add cheese, blend and serve immediately.

RISOTTO WITH PEAS

READY TRAY   Serves 4 to 6

2 slices bacon, finely chopped
4 tablespoons butter
1 cup rice
   Salt and pepper
3 cups broth
½ pound fresh or frozen peas
4 tablespoons grated Parmesan cheese

59

Sauté bacon lightly in 2 tablespoons of butter. Add rice and stir until liquid is absorbed. Salt and pepper to taste, add broth and stir gently until it comes to a boil.

Pour into a casserole, bake uncovered in 350° oven for approximately 20 minutes.

Meanwhile, place 2 tablespoons butter in a saucepan. Add fresh or frozen peas, a little broth, salt and pepper lightly, cover and cook slowly until barely tender.

Add peas to casserole, blend and bake for 10 to 15 minutes.

Sprinkle with cheese before serving.

MUSHROOM RISOTTO

READY TRAY   Serves 4 to 6

3   tablespoons olive oil
1   onion, finely chopped
1   clove garlic, finely chopped
1   stalk celery, finely chopped
1   carrot, finely chopped
1   tablespoon parsley, finely chopped
½   pound fresh mushrooms, cut into ½-inch pieces
1   cup rice
4   tablespoons tomato sauce
    Hot broth or water
    Salt and pepper
4   tablespoons butter
4   tablespoons grated Parmesan cheese

Sauté in oil the onion, garlic, celery, carrot and parsley until golden brown. Add mushrooms and sauté until they begin to wilt, stirring gently. Add rice and stir until liquid is absorbed.

Blend tomato sauce with enough hot broth or water to make 3 cups of liquid. Add to rice, season to taste with salt and pepper, and bring to slow boil, stirring gently. Pour into a large casserole, bake uncovered in 350° oven for 30 minutes or until liquid is absorbed and rice is tender.

Add butter and cheese, blending thoroughly before serving.

SHRIMP RISOTTO WITH CAPERS

Serves 4 to 6

½   *pound fresh shrimps, shelled and cleaned*
½   *cup butter*
1   *onion, finely chopped*
2   *cloves garlic, finely chopped*
2   *stalks celery, finely chopped*
1   *tablespoon parsley, finely chopped*
1   *cup rice*
   Salt and pepper
1   *small can (8 ounces) tomato sauce*
   Hot broth or water
2   *tablespoons drained capers*
4   *tablespoons grated Parmesan cheese*

Sauté in butter the onion, garlic, celery and parsley. When onion begins to brown, add shrimp and sauté 5 minutes. Add rice, salt and pepper to taste, and continue stirring until liquid is absorbed.

Blend tomato sauce with enough hot broth or water to make 3 cups of liquid. Add to rice with capers, stir until it comes to a boil.

Pour into a casserole, bake uncovered in 350° oven for 30 to 40 minutes, or until liquid is absorbed and rice is flaky and tender.

Sprinkle with cheese before serving.

Beef

Nothing can surpass the classic prime ribs of beef or thick steak roasted or broiled unadorned, to permit the rich, good flavor of the beef to be enjoyed to the utmost. The recipes in this chapter suggest ways to add new flavors to lesser cuts of beef or to vary roasts and steaks.

Here are some hints for preparing steak. Try rubbing the steak well with oil before broiling. The heat will char the oil not the steak and seal in the juices.

A good marinade for steak is a mixture of 1 tablespoon wine vinegar and 2 tablespoons oil or melted butter, a clove of crushed garlic and herbs of your choice. Leave steak in the marinade for several hours before cooking, turning several times.

For top-of-stove broiling, preheat a heavy skillet until very hot. Sprinkle a thin layer of salt over the bottom of the pan and sear the steak quickly to seal in the juices. Then cook to desired doneness.

BOILED BEEF DELIGHT

READY TRAY   Serves 4

2   pounds boiling beef
¼   pound salt pork, chopped fine
1   onion, chopped fine
1   carrot, chopped fine
2   stalks celery, chopped fine
1   small can (8 ounces) tomato sauce
6   dried mushrooms, soaked, drained and chopped fine
     Salt and pepper
     Broth from boiled beef
2   tablespoons butter
1   tablespoon parsley, chopped fine

Place beef in salted water to cover, and simmer until tender, approximately 2 hours.

Render salt pork in a heavy skillet. Discard salt pork and in same skillet sauté onion, carrot, celery, until wilted. Add boiled beef, tomato sauce and mushrooms, with salt and pepper to taste, cover and simmer until mushrooms are tender and sauce is smooth. If sauce be-

comes too thick, thin with a small amount of broth.
When ready to serve, add butter to the sauce and blend.
Place meat on serving platter, sprinkle with parsley
before slicing. Serve the sauce separately.

GRANDMOTHER'S BOILED BEEF

READY TRAY   Serves 4

12   *fresh green onions, chopped fine*
 6   *tablespoons butter*
 1   *large clove garlic, chopped fine*
 2   *pounds cold boiled beef, sliced ¼ inch thick*
     Salt and pepper
 2   *cups broth*
     Juice of ½ fresh lemon
 1   *tablespoon parsley, chopped fine*

In a heavy skillet sauté onions in butter until golden
brown. Add garlic, meat, salt and pepper to taste. Add
broth, a small amount at a time, as the meat absorbs
the liquid. Simmer until the meat is thoroughly heated
and liquid is reduced to a thick sauce.

Remove meat to platter, sprinkle with lemon juice
and parsley before serving.

BEEF CROQUETTES

READY TRAY   Serves 4

½   *pound ground beef*
½   *pound sweet Italian sausages, casings removed*
½   *large clove garlic, finely chopped*
 2   *tablespoons parsley, finely chopped*
     Salt
     Black pepper
 3   *slices white bread, soaked in milk and squeezed dry*
 1   *egg, beaten*
     Breadcrumbs
     Olive oil

Combine all ingredients except the last two, and blend
well. Shape into small croquettes, roll in breadcrumbs
and sauté in oil until well browned on both sides.

63

BEEF CUTLETS

Serves 4

1½   pounds round steak, ½ inch thick
⅛   pound prosciutto, chopped fine
1   onion, chopped fine
1   clove garlic, minced
1   stalk celery, chopped fine
1   carrot, chopped fine
1   tablespoon parsley, chopped fine
     Salt and pepper
4   tablespoons butter
1   tablespoon olive oil
2   tablespoons tomato paste, diluted with equal amount of broth
½   cup red wine

> Pound steak well and cut into pieces 3 inches square.
> Mix prosciutto, onion, garlic, celery, carrot, parsley, and salt and pepper to taste. Spread on the cutlets, roll and tie with heavy thread.
> Melt butter and oil in a casserole and place the cutlets in it. Bake uncovered in 350° oven. When they begin to brown, add the tomato paste and wine, cover and continue baking until cutlets are tender.

BEEF CUTLETS WITH MUSHROOMS

READY TRAY   Serves 4 to 6

1½   pounds sirloin tip, ½ inch thick, cut in 3-inch squares
1   teaspoon allspice
½   teaspoon powdered marjoram
1   onion, chopped fine
1   tablespoon olive oil
     Salt and pepper
¼   cup red wine
1   tablespoon tomato paste
½   cup broth
2   tablespoons butter
1   pound fresh mushrooms, thinly sliced
1   clove garlic, chopped fine
1   tablespoon parsley, chopped fine

> Flatten cutlets with broad side of a heavy knife. Blend allspice and marjoram and rub into cutlets. In a heavy

64

skillet heat oil and sauté onion until wilted. Add cutlets, with salt and pepper to taste, browning them slowly. Add wine and when it is absorbed, add tomato paste and broth. Simmer until tender.

In another skillet sauté mushrooms, garlic and parsley in 2 tablespoons butter until wilted. Add 4 tablespoons broth and salt to taste.

Remove cutlets to serving platter. Add mushrooms to meat juices, blend well and pour over cutlets before serving.

BEEF ROLLATINE

Serves 4

1½ *pounds round steak or sirloin tip, in one slice, ½ inch thick*
 2 *tablespoons butter*
 1 *tablespoon olive oil*
 1 *onion, chopped fine*
 2 *stalks celery, chopped fine*
 1 *carrot, chopped fine*
 ½ *pound lean veal, chopped fine*
 2 *chicken livers, chopped fine*
 2 *tablespoons parsley, chopped fine*
    Salt and pepper
    Breadcrumbs
 ⅛ *pound prosciutto, chopped fine*
 4 *tablespoons grated Parmesan cheese*
 1 *egg, beaten lightly*
 ⅔ *cup tomato sauce*
 ¼ *cup broth*

To prepare filling, heat butter and oil in heavy skillet. Add onion, celery, carrot, veal, chicken livers and sauté lightly. Add parsley, and salt and pepper to taste. Brown well, adding enough broth to prevent burning. Remove from heat, add prosciutto and cheese and blend thoroughly. Put through a fine grinder. Add egg and a few breadcrumbs, if needed, to produce a smooth blend.

Flatten round steak with broad side of a large knife. Place filling in center of the steak lengthwise. Roll and tie with heavy thread 1½ inches apart. Sear well on all sides in a little butter or oil. Add tomato sauce, broth, cover and roast in 350° oven for 1½ hours, or until tender.

Remove thread before slicing. Serve with strained sauce from roasting pan.

BEEF ROLLATINE WITH ANCHOVY

Serves 4

1½   pounds lean beef, sliced thin, cut in 3-inch squares
⅛   pound prosciutto, chopped fine
4   anchovy fillets, chopped fine
2   tablespoons parsley, chopped fine
4   tablespoons butter
       Pepper
⅓   cup white wine
⅓   cup broth

Flatten each cutlet with the broad side of a large knife.

Blend thoroughly the prosciutto, anchovies and parsley. Spread thinly over each cutlet, roll and tie with thread or secure with a toothpick.

Melt butter in a large skillet and put in beef rolls in a single layer. Season to taste with pepper only. Brown lightly on all sides, add wine, cover and cook over medium-low heat. When cooked on one side, turn and add broth, cover and cook until tender. Almost all the pan juices will be absorbed by the meat when it is ready to serve.

Remove thread or toothpicks before serving.

ROAST BEEF IN SKILLET

Serves 4 to 6

3   pounds sirloin of beef, cut in lengthwise piece
3   tablespoons olive oil
4   tablespoons butter
1   clove garlic, gently pressed
1   sprig fresh rosemary
       Salt and pepper
⅓   cup white wine
6   tablespoons tomato sauce
¼   cup broth

Tie meat at 1½-inch intervals. Place in a heavy skillet with oil, butter, garlic and rosemary. Brown over high heat quickly on all sides, turning often. Salt and pepper to taste. Add wine, cover and cook 5 minutes. Add tomato sauce, broth, cover and cook over medium heat to desired tenderness.

Remove meat to serving platter, and serve with own sauce.

BEEF FILLETS WITH PROSCIUTTO

Serves 4

2   *pounds beef fillets, ½ inch thick*
1   *egg*
    Pepper
    Breadcrumbs
¼   *pound thinly sliced prosciutto*
¼   *pound thinly sliced mozzarella cheese*
4   *tablespoons butter*
2   *tablespoons olive oil*
½   *cup white wine*

Beat egg with pepper until light. Dip fillets in beaten egg, then in breadcrumbs. Place a slice of prosciutto on each fillet, and a slice of cheese on top of the prosciutto.

Melt butter with oil in a large oven-proof dish, and place the fillets in a single layer in the dish. Place in 350° oven, uncovered. After 15 minutes, pour wine around the fillets, being careful not to get any on the fillets. Cook 15 minutes longer. These are at their best served medium rare.

ROAST BEEF WITH PROSCIUTTO

Serves 4 to 6

3   *pounds sirloin of beef*
4   *thin slices prosciutto, rather fat*
1   *onion, quartered*
1   *stalk celery, cut in 1-inch pieces*
1   *carrot, cut in 1-inch pieces*
4   *tablespoons butter*
    Salt and pepper
1   *cup broth or water*

Place prosciutto over beef and tie together 1½ inches apart, forming a cylinder.

67

Place onion, celery, carrot and butter in a roasting pan, and add beef. Salt and pepper to taste, but use salt sparingly since the prosciutto is salty.

Roast uncovered in 350° oven 30 minutes, turn the meat, add broth or water, and continue roasting to desired tenderness.

Place meat on serving platter and serve with pan juices which have been strained. A thicker gravy may be made by diluting 1 tablespoon cornstarch with a little water, and adding it to the strained pan juices. Cook over low heat, stirring continuously until smooth.

BEEF FILLETS IN MARSALA

READY TRAY   Serves 4

4   fillets of beef, ¾ inch thick
4   tablespoons butter
4   slices toast, buttered, trimmed and cut in triangles
    Salt and pepper
Sauce
2   tablespoons butter
2   tablespoons flour
¼   cup Marsala wine
4   dried mushrooms, boiled, drained and chopped fine;
    reserve water in which mushrooms were boiled
    Salt

Flatten the fillets with the broad side of a large knife and set aside.

Place 2 tablespoons butter in small saucepan and blend in flour until smooth. Add wine, mushrooms with reserved liquid, and salt to taste. Cook over low heat until sauce is of a smooth consistency. If needed, add a small amount of broth.

Brown meat in 4 tablespoons butter. Salt and pepper to taste. The fillets should be cooked quickly to medium-rare stage. Place on toast triangles, and pour sauce over them.

BUTTERFLY STEAK VESUVIO

Butterfly Steak Vesuvio is a tenderloin or filet, weighing about 12 ounces, split down the center to a thickness of

68

about ¼ to ½ inch throughout, and with about ¼ inch of fat left on the outer edge.

2 *tenderloin or filet steaks, butterflied by butcher*
2 *tablespoons olive oil*
2 *tablespoons melted butter*
2 *green onions, chopped fine*
12 *fresh medium-size mushrooms, thinly sliced*
¼ *cup A-1 sauce*
¼ *cup pale dry sherry wine*
   Salt and freshly ground black pepper
2 *tablespoons Cognac or brandy*

Prepare steak by searing in oil to desired doneness in a crepe pan over a high flame, or in an electric fry pan, or in a fry pan over high heat. Do not season meat at this time. Keep hot on hot dinner plates.

To prepare sauce, simmer melted butter in the same pan over high heat, and when bubbling, add onions, mushrooms, A-1 sauce, salt and pepper to taste, and sauté lightly. Add wine and blend thoroughly. Place steaks back in pan with sauce and heat through. Pour Cognac or brandy into pan and ignite. Serve immediately.

PEPPER STEAK

READY TRAY   Serves 4

1 *New York steak, 1½ inches thick, cut into ¼-inch slices*
2 *tablespoons peppercorns, coarsely ground*
2 *tablespoons butter*
2 *cloves shallots or garlic, finely chopped*
½ *cup dry white wine*
2 *tablespoons brandy*
1 *teaspoon butter*
   Salt

Cover both sides of meat generously with ground peppercorns. Pound pepper firmly into meat, using a potato masher or the underside of the bowl of a large spoon.

In a large-size crepe pan over direct high flame, or in electric fry pan, or a fry pan over high heat, brown both

sides of meat in the butter and shallots or garlic. Sauté
to desired degree of rareness and transfer to hot plates.

Add wine and brandy to the pan juices and simmer
for several minutes. Add butter and pour the sauce,
including pepper, over the steaks and serve immediately.
If anyone wants to season the meat with salt—let him!

Veal

The Italians use more veal than beef and have become masters in its preparation. True veal is meat from a milk-fed calf, not more than three months old when it is prepared for market. The meat is pink and firm and the bones hard.

Many of the recipes that follow call for veal scallops. The best come from the tenderloin but are difficult to obtain, so scallops cut from the leg are usually used. The scallop can be identified easily because it is quite pronounced, being surrounded by a thin membrane of tissue. Gently separate the natural scallop from the membrane and the meat around it for use in other dishes. To tenderize the small scallops, pound, flatten and smooth them out until very thin, using the broad side of a heavy knife.

Although veal should never be served rare, it is important not to overcook it or it will be dry and tasteless. It is a meat that is just as delicious cold as hot, and when prepared in advance, it is equally flavorful on reheating.

Veal stock is made in the same way as beef stock, usually taking less time. While the stock will not be as rich, it has a delicate and superior flavor which gives character to sauces that require a white rather than brown stock.

VEAL CHOPS, MILANESE

READY TRAY   Serves 6

6   veal loin chops, trimmed
⅛   pound prosciutto, finely chopped
⅛   pound button mushrooms, finely chopped
1   tablespoon parsley, finely chopped
2   tablespoons grated Parmesan cheese
    Salt and pepper
2   eggs, lightly beaten
    Breadcrumbs
    Butter
    Lemon wedges

Flatten chops with broad side of a heavy knife.
Blend to a smooth paste in a mortar with pestle or in an electric blender, the prosciutto, mushrooms, parsley,

71

cheese, salt and pepper to taste. Spread paste evenly over one side of each chop.

Dip chops very carefully in beaten egg, then into breadcrumbs, patting gently with the palm of hand.

Sauté in plenty of butter until golden brown.

Serve with lemon wedges.

VEAL CUTLETS À LA MARTINESE

READY TRAY   Serves 4

1	pound veal cutlets, sliced thin
1	egg, lightly beaten
2	tablespoons parsley, finely chopped
3	tablespoons grated Parmesan cheese
1	clove garlic, minced
	Salt and pepper
	Breadcrumbs
1	onion, finely chopped
2	cloves garlic, finely chopped
4	tablespoons butter
1	small can (8 ounces) tomato sauce
	Broth

Flatten cutlets with broad side of a heavy knife. Combine egg, parsley, cheese, minced garlic, salt and pepper to taste and enough breadcrumbs to make a smooth, thick paste.

Spread paste thinly over one side of each cutlet; roll and tie with heavy thread or secure with toothpicks.

Sauté onion and chopped garlic in butter until golden brown. Add cutlets and brown on all sides. Add tomato sauce and a small amount of broth, cover and simmer 40 minutes until tender.

VEAL MARSALA

READY TRAY   Serves 4 to 6

1½	pounds veal, cut very thin
	Flour
	Salt and pepper
4	tablespoons butter
½	cup Marsala wine

72

Flatten meat with broad side of a heavy knife. Flour lightly and salt and pepper to taste.

Brown meat in butter thoroughly. Add wine and heat thoroughly, about 2 minutes. Serve immediately.

Sliced mushrooms and a few herbs of your choice may also be added for an excellent variation.

VEAL CUTLETS, MARSALA

READY TRAY   Serves 4

½   *pound fresh button mushrooms, sliced thin*
6   *tablespoons butter*
1   *pound veal cutlets, ¼ inch thick*
   Salt and pepper
   Flour
¼   *cup Marsala wine*

Sauté mushrooms lightly in 2 tablespoons butter for 5 minutes. Set aside.

Flatten cutlets with the broad side of a heavy knife. Salt and pepper to taste, flour lightly, and sauté in 4 tablespoons butter until golden brown. Add wine, cover and simmer 5 minutes.

Place cutlets on heated serving platter.

In pan in which cutlets were cooked, heat sautéed mushrooms thoroughly and serve over cutlets.

GROUND VEAL CUTLETS

READY TRAY   Serves 4

2   *eggs, lightly beaten*
1   *pound lean veal, put through fine grinder twice*
1   *clove garlic, chopped fine*
2   *tablespoons grated Parmesan cheese*
   Pinch ground nutmeg
   Flour
   Salt and pepper
   Breadcrumbs
   Juice of 1 whole lemon
   Butter
   Broth

Combine thoroughly eggs, ground veal, garlic, cheese, nutmeg, 1 tablespoon flour, salt and pepper to taste. Add a few breadcrumbs, if needed, to absorb excess liquid, or add a small amount of broth if too dry.

Shape into small cutlets. Flour lightly and sauté in butter until golden brown on both sides. Set aside and keep warm.

Blend 1 tablespoon flour with lemon juice until smooth. Add to pan in which cutlets were cooked, adding butter and enough broth to make a smooth gravy. Serve over cutlets.

MAMA'S VEAL KIDNEY CHOPS

READY TRAY   Serves 2

4   thick veal kidney chops
    Salt and pepper
    Flour
    Rosemary leaves
    Oil
½   cup white wine

Season chops lightly with salt and pepper. Dust with flour.

Place chops in skillet with a little rosemary sprinkled over the top. Sauté in oil slowly until browned on one side, turn, add wine and brown other side. The chops should be cooked for about 30 minutes. Pour pan juices over chops before serving.

BROILED VEAL KIDNEY CHOPS

READY TRAY   Serves 2

2   double veal rib kidney chops
6   tablespoons melted butter
    Salt and pepper
    Lemon wedges

Split chops halfway and open flat into butterfly shape. Brush with butter and season to taste with pepper.

Place under broiler, brown both sides. Do not over-broil.

Season to taste with salt before serving. Place a pat of butter on top of each chop and garnish with lemon wedges.

SALTIMBOCCA VICTOR

Saltimbocca was made famous by the La Tosca Restaurant in Milan, Italy, around the corner from La Scala Opera House. There it was prepared in bite-size cigar-shaped rolls, and the ladies who frequented the restaurant before or after the opera could pick them up with their fingers and drop them into their mouths without smearing their lipstick. Hence the name Saltimbocca—"jump in the mouth." Today the cutlets are left flat, not rolled.

READY TRAY   Serves 4

10   *veal scallops, 1/4 inch thick, cut from leg of veal*
     Salt and freshly ground black pepper
     Fresh rosemary leaves
1/4 *pound prosciutto, sliced very thin*
1/4 *pound mozzarella cheese*
4   *tablespoons butter*
1/3 *cup sherry wine*
1/3 *cup Burgundy wine*
1/3 *cup sauterne wine*
1/4 *pound mushrooms, sliced thin*

Flatten veal scallops as thin as possible to 3-inch squares, using broad side of a heavy knife. Salt and pepper to taste, using salt sparingly.

Place a few rosemary leaves over center of meat. Cut prosciutto to same size as veal and place on top of each square. Cover with thin slice of cheese, and tie squares crosswise or secure with toothpicks.

Brown in butter quickly, cheese side up.

Combine wines and add to skillet with mushrooms. Cover, reduce heat and simmer 20 minutes or until tender.

Remove thread or toothpicks before serving. Serve cheese side up, with pan sauce.

VEAL SCALOPPINE IN CREAM

READY TRAY   Serves 4

1   pound veal scaloppine, ¼ inch thick, cut in 2-inch squares
    Salt and pepper
    Flour
4   tablespoons butter
½   cup fresh cream
    Broth

Flatten veal scallops with broad side of a heavy knife. Salt and pepper to taste and dust lightly with flour. Sauté quickly in butter until golden brown.

Add cream and a small amount of broth. Cover and simmer over low heat 30 minutes. Remove meat to heated serving platter.

Thicken liquid in pan by adding 1 tablespoon butter, blended with 1 tablespoon flour, stirring until smooth. Serve over scaloppine.

COLD VEAL AND TUNA

READY TRAY   Serves 4

2   pounds milk-fed veal, in one thick piece
3   whole cloves
1   small onion, peeled
2   stalks celery, cut in 2-inch pieces
2   carrots, cut in 2-inch pieces
4   sprigs fresh parsley
1   bay leaf
    Salt and pepper
1   small can tuna
4   anchovy fillets
2   tablespoons olive oil
    Juice of 1 whole lemon
2   tablespoons pickled capers
    Lemon wedges

Insert cloves into onion and place in kettle with veal, celery, carrot, parsley and bay leaf. Add salt and pepper to taste and water to cover. Cover and simmer over low heat 1 hour until tender. Remove meat and cool thoroughly.

Thoroughly mash tuna and anchovies with fork. Slowly add oil and lemon juice, blending until smooth.

Place cold veal in a deep dish and pour tuna-anchovy sauce over it. Sprinkle with capers and set in refrigerator 24 hours before serving so that the salsa permeates the meat.

Cut in thin slices, serve with salsa and lemon wedges.

VEAL SCALOPPINE, BOLOGNESE

READY TRAY   Serves 6

2   pounds veal scallops, 1/4 inch thick
2   tablespoons butter
1/4 pound prosciutto, thinly sliced
1/4 pound mozzarella cheese, thinly sliced
    Pepper
    Juice of 1 whole lemon

Flatten veal scallops with broad side of a heavy knife, until very thin.

Butter the bottom of a shallow baking dish, large enough to hold the meat in a single layer. Place prosciutto and cheese in layers over meat, sprinkling a little lemon juice over each layer. Dot with butter and season to taste with pepper only.

Bake uncovered in 350° oven 45 minutes until tender.

VEAL SCALOPPINE, PROVENÇALE

READY TRAY   Serves 2

10 veal scallops, cut from leg of milk-fed baby veal, 1/4 inch thick,
    2 inches square
    Flour
    Salt and freshly ground black pepper
4   teaspoons butter
2   teaspoons olive oil
6   fresh or canned mushrooms, sliced
1/2 cucumber, diced
1   tomato, diced
2   tablespoons chives, chopped fine
1   teaspoon garlic butter, made by adding 2 cloves of finely chopped
    garlic to butter and blending well
2   tablespoons Marsala or sherry wine

77

Flatten veal squares with broad side of a heavy knife. Flour lightly, season to taste with salt and pepper.

Make crepe pan, electric fry pan or fry pan very hot over direct flame or heat. Melt butter and add oil. Sauté meat, quickly browning both sides. Remove meat from pan and keep warm.

To prepare sauce: Place mushrooms in pan, add cucumbers, tomatoes, chives and garlic butter, and sauté over hot flame or heat 2 minutes. Add wine and blend well. Pour sauce over veal and serve hot.

(If fresh mushrooms are used, place in pan first when preparing sauce. If canned mushrooms are used, place in pan after tomatoes have been added.)

VEAL OSSO BUCO

Osso buco means "bone with a hole through the center," which is the veal shank.

Serves 4 to 6

4	*veal shanks, cut in 2-inch pieces, with marrow*
1	*onion, finely chopped*
2	*stalks celery, finely chopped*
1	*carrot, finely chopped*
4	*tablespoons butter*
2	*tablespoons olive oil*
½	*cup white wine*
6	*dried mushrooms soaked, drained and chopped*
¾	*cup tomato sauce or canned tomatoes*
1	*cup broth*
	Salt and pepper
1	*tablespoon parsley, finely chopped*
1	*teaspoon grated lemon peel*

Sauté shanks, onion, celery and carrot in butter and oil until well browned. Add wine, cover and cook over medium heat 5 minutes. Add mushrooms, tomato sauce or tomatoes, broth, salt and pepper to taste. Cover and cook over medium heat until tender.

Remove shanks from pan. Strain sauce and put it back in the pan with the shanks, adding chopped parsley and lemon peel. Simmer for 5 minutes and serve.

POTTED VEAL

Serves 4 to 6

2   *pounds veal round steak, cut in thick piece*
2   *thin slices prosciutto*
4   *tablespoons butter*
1   *onion, quartered*
1   *carrot, cut in 2-inch pieces*
1   *stalk celery, cut in 2-inch pieces*
4   *sprigs fresh parsley*
4   *whole cloves*
    Salt and pepper
    Broth
    Oil

Place prosciutto over meat. Roll and tie meat together at 1½-inch intervals, forming a cylinder.

Place in casserole with butter, onion, carrot, celery, parsley, cloves, salt and pepper to taste. Use salt sparingly since the prosciutto is salty.

Brown veal in oil on all sides, adding a small amount of broth, as needed, to keep it a little moist. Cover and simmer over low heat 1½ hours or until tender.

Remove cover during the last 15 minutes to allow liquid to concentrate a little. Strain and serve over meat.

ROAST LEG OF VEAL, LARDED

Serves 6

1   *boned leg of veal, about 3 pounds*
¼   *pound salt pork, cut in thick strips*
3   *slices prosciutto, rolled*
2   *cloves garlic, quartered*
    Salt and freshly ground black pepper
1   *teaspoon monosodium glutamate*
½   *teaspoon nutmeg*
    Fresh or dried basil
¼   *cup olive oil*
½   *cup tomato sauce*
½   *cup sherry wine*

Roll and tie veal 1½ inches apart. Lard meat with salt pork and prosciutto. The butcher may do this for you, but if you have a larding needle, try doing it yourself.

Cut slits in meat with sharp paring knife and insert garlic pieces. Combine salt and pepper to taste, monosodium glutamate and nutmeg, and rub well into meat. Place in casserole, sprinkle with basil and oil. Mix tomato sauce and wine and add to casserole.

Roast in 350° oven for 1 hour, basting with juice. Reduce temperature to 300° and roast 30 minutes longer or until tender. Add more tomato sauce and wine, as needed, to prevent dryness.

VEAL ROLL-UPS WITH CAPERS

READY TRAY   Serves 4 to 6

2   *tablespoons pitted ripe olives, finely chopped*
2   *tablespoons pickled capers, drained and finely chopped*
2   *anchovy fillets, finely chopped*
1   *tablespoon grated Parmesan cheese*
1   *egg yolk, lightly beaten*
1½ *pounds veal cutlets, ¼ inch thick, cut in 2-inch pieces*
2   *tablespoons olive oil*
1   *onion, finely chopped*
4   *tablespoons butter*
    Pepper
2   *tablespoons white wine*
2   *tablespoons tomato paste, diluted with equal amount of broth*

Combine olives, capers, anchovies, cheese and egg yolk in a mortar with a pestle, or in an electric blender, reducing to a thick paste.

Flatten cutlets with broad side of a heavy knife and brush lightly with oil. Spread paste thinly over each cutlet. Roll and tie with heavy thread or secure with toothpicks.

Brown onions and veal roll-ups in butter. Season to taste with pepper. Add wine and diluted tomato paste. Cover and simmer 45 minutes until tender, turning occasionally.

Lamb

Spring lamb is a traditional Easter dish in Italy. The aroma of lamb, sprinkled with herbs and turning slowly over a fire of pine boughs, would announce the end of the austerities of the Lenten season. The taste of baby lamb is the taste of spring itself, with a flavor as delicate and mild as a gentle breeze over a bed of tulips.

Lamb is always best cooked at low heat and should be cooked until well done, but still pink and juicy. Use rosemary, garlic and wine for added flavor.

BABY LAMB ON SPIT OR BROILED

Just as it is customary to serve turkey at Thanksgiving, so it is customary for the Italians to serve baby lamb or kid at Easter time. Kid, or baby goat, known as *capretto*, is used throughout the whole Mediterranean region, and it can be prepared in the same manner as baby lamb.

READY TRAY   Serves 6 to 8

1   *baby lamb, or any part of it*
½   *cup olive oil*
1   *teaspoon dried rosemary*
1   *clove garlic, gently crushed*
    Salt and pepper
1   *teaspoon wine vinegar*

Blend thoroughly oil, rosemary, garlic, salt and pepper to taste and vinegar.

Place meat on a large tray and puncture in many places with a sharp paring knife. Brush meat with the marinade at intervals for several hours before cooking. Place meat on spit or in large roasting pan, and cook in moderate oven for approximately 1 hour or until tender. Baste often while roasting. If needed, prepare additional basting sauce.

81

ROAST LEG OF LAMB

Serves 6 to 8

1   5 to 6 pound leg of lamb, boned, tied and fell removed
2   cloves garlic, cut in half
¼   cup olive oil
     Salt and pepper
2   stalks celery, cut in 1-inch pieces
2   carrots, cut in 1-inch pieces
2   sprigs fresh rosemary
     Hot water
2   tablespoons flour

Make deep slits in meat with sharp paring knife and insert garlic. Rub meat on all sides with oil, and salt and pepper to taste. Cover bottom of roasting pan with celery and carrots. Place meat on it and add rosemary sprigs.

Roast uncovered in 350° oven until tender, allowing 30 minutes per pound. Brown meat on all sides, then add a small amount of hot water to pan for basting. When roast is done, place on serving platter and let set at least 15 minutes before carving.

Strain liquid and return to roasting pan. Add 1 cup water, bring to boil. Blend flour with ⅓ cup water and add to boiling liquid, stirring until smooth and of desired consistency. Salt and pepper to taste. Serve with the roast.

LOIN OF LAMB, PARMESAN

READY TRAY   Serves 4

2   pounds loin of lamb, cut in small pieces
4   tablespoons olive oil
2   cloves garlic, minced
1   tablespoon parsley, finely chopped
     Salt and pepper
¼   cup white wine
     Broth
2   egg yolks, lightly beaten
4   tablespoons grated Parmesan cheese
     Juice of 1 whole lemon

In a heavy skillet brown lamb well in oil. Add garlic, parsley, salt and pepper to taste. When garlic is golden, add wine and cook covered for 5 minutes.

Add a small amount of broth to prevent dryness, cover and cook over medium heat until tender.

Blend egg yolks, cheese and lemon juice until smooth. Add to lamb, stir well and simmer until sauce is smooth.

LAMB SHOULDER ALL'UMIDO

Serves 4 to 6

All'umido literally means "with dampness." It is the Italian method of cooking meats with very little liquid, in order to keep the juices and flavors in the meat.

6   *green onions, sliced thin*
6   *tablespoons butter*
1   *shoulder of lamb, 4 to 5 pounds*
    Salt and pepper
2   *tablespoons flour*
    Broth

In 4 tablespoons butter sauté onions until golden brown. Add lamb, salt and pepper to taste, cover and cook slowly until browned and tender. Turn often and add a little broth, as needed.

Blend remainder of butter with flour until smooth and add to meat with a little broth. Cook until thoroughly blended.

POACHED LEG OF LAMB WITH CAPER SAUCE

Serves 6 to 8

 1 *leg of lamb, 5 to 6 pounds, fell removed*
    Salt
12 *small white onions*
12 *small carrots*
12 *small turnips*
 4 *tablespoons butter*
 3 *tablespoons flour*
 3 *cups strained lamb broth*
½   *cup capers with juice*

Wrap meat lightly in a linen cloth and sew securely. Place in a deep roasting pan and pour over enough boiling water to cover. Place roasting pan on top of stove over high heat and bring to a boil. Cover, reduce heat and simmer slowly for 1 hour. Add salt to taste and simmer 1 hour longer until tender.

Boil onions, carrots and turnips in salted water until tender.

Remove cloth from meat and place on large platter. Arrange cooked vegetables around the meat.

Melt 3 tablespoons butter and blend in flour thoroughly. Gradually stir in lamb broth until smooth. Add capers and juice. Just before serving, add 1 tablespoon butter. Serve sauce separately.

LOIN OF LAMB WITH GREEN BEANS

READY TRAY   Serves 4

2   *pounds loin of lamb, cut into 1½-inch pieces*
2   *tablespoons olive oil*
2   *cloves garlic, gently crushed*
2   *pinches rosemary*
¼   *cup red wine*
½   *cup tomato sauce*
     Salt and pepper
     Broth
1   *pound green beans, in 3-inch pieces, cooked and drained*
4   *tablespoons butter*

In a heavy skillet brown lamb on all sides in oil, with garlic and rosemary. Add wine and cook covered for 5 minutes. Add tomato sauce, salt and pepper to taste. Cover and cook over medium heat until tender. As sauce thickens, thin out with a small amount of broth.

Place meat on heated platter. Add cooked beans and butter to pan, and cook until sauce is almost absorbed. Serve beans and lamb separately.

Any fresh green vegetable is very good prepared in this manner.

84

LAMB AND ANCHOVIES

Serves 4 to 6

2 *pounds lean lamb, cut in 1-inch pieces*
2 *tablespoons olive oil*
   Salt and pepper
½ *cup red wine*
¼ *cup broth*
4 *anchovy fillets*
2 *cloves garlic, finely chopped*
½ *teaspoon ground rosemary*
1 *tablespoon parsley, finely chopped*

> Brown meat in oil. Lightly salt and pepper to taste. Add ¼ cup wine and broth, cover and simmer 45 minutes until tender.
>
> Mash thoroughly the anchovies, garlic and rosemary. Blend in remainder of wine. Add to meat and cook over high heat uncovered for 5 minutes. Sprinkle with parsley and serve.

ROAST RACK OF LAMB

READY TRAY   Serves 4 to 6

1 *rack of lamb, 6 to 8 chops*
   Salt and pepper
   Butter
12 *small new potatoes*
2 *Italian truffles, sliced thin*

> Rub meat well with salt and pepper to taste and butter. Roast uncovered in 325° oven until tender, allowing 15 minutes per pound.
>
> Peel and slice potatoes and sauté in 3 tablespoons butter until tender and golden brown on both sides. Salt and pepper to taste, carefully stir in truffles and sauté 3 minutes.
>
> Place roasted rack of lamb on heated serving platter and surround with potato and truffle slices.
>
> Skim fat from roaster and serve pan juices over meat.

Pork

Many of the recipes in this book call for prosciutto. This is ham that has been cured in the Italian manner. It is a lean whole ham of a rich pale red color. All of the juices have been pressed out of it, and it is aged in spices, particularly coarsely ground black pepper, which produces a more concentrated flavor than ordinary boiled ham.

It is best when sliced paper thin, either lengthwise or across the grain. Small quantities are usually purchased because it is expensive and best used fresh. If it remains in the refrigerator too long, it will dry out and become brittle and gritty with salt.

The varieties of dried Italian sausages that are obtainable at any delicatessen or store specializing in sausages are many; they include salami, peperoni, salsiccia secca, capocollo, bologna. Homemade sausage has an entirely different flavor and you might want to try making your own. Two recipes are included.

SWEET SAUSAGE, ITALIAN STYLE

READY TRAY

2   *pounds lean pork*
1   *pound fat pork*
3   *teaspoons salt*
2   *teaspoons fennel seeds*
2   *cloves garlic*
½   *teaspoon freshly ground black pepper*
1   *teaspoon finely chopped red chili peppers*
    Casings

Grind lean and fat pork, using fine blade of the food chopper. Blend salt, fennel seeds and garlic together in a mortar until smooth. Add to meat along with both peppers and mix thoroughly. Fill casings.

Casings can be obtained from butcher. The salted casings must be soaked in warm water for several hours, then rinsed in running water thoroughly. At the same time pour a cup of vinegar through the casing so the sausage will keep better.

Cut casing in to 2-foot lengths for easier handling. Tie one end and fill with prepared sausage meat, using a funnel or a sausage-stuffing machine, if one is available. Then tie in lengths of 4 to 8 inches. Loop links over a clothes hanger and dry 4 hours before refrigerating.

PORK CHOPS AND PEPPERS

READY TRAY   Serves 3

1 *clove garlic, gently crushed*
2 *tablespoons olive oil*
6 *pork loin chops*
   Salt and pepper
1 *tablespoon tomato paste*
2 *tablespoons broth or water*
2 *fresh sweet peppers, seeded, cut in 1-inch strips*
⅓ *pound fresh mushrooms, sliced thin*
                    or
6 *dried mushrooms, soaked, drained and sliced*

Brown garlic in oil and discard. Brown chops well in the oil. Salt and pepper to taste.

Add tomato paste, diluted with broth or water, and peppers and mushrooms. Cover and simmer 30 minutes until tender.

Add a little broth or water as the sauce thickens.

PORK LOIN CHOPS IN WINE

READY TRAY   Serves 4

4 *pork loin chops, 1½ inches thick, boned and trimmed*
2 *tablespoons olive oil*
   Salt and pepper
½ *cup white wine*
4 *tablespoons tomato sauce*
4 *tablespoons broth or hot water*

In a heavy skillet, brown chops in oil on both sides. Drain fat, add salt and pepper to taste and wine, cover and simmer over low heat until wine is almost absorbed, turning chops occasionally.

Blend tomato sauce with broth or hot water and add to chops. Cover and simmer 30 minutes until tender.

Do not let sauce become completely absorbed, adding a small amount of broth or hot water to prevent dryness. Serve a little of the sauce over each chop.

ROAST PORK LOIN

READY TRAY   Serves 4 to 6

1   *pork loin, 3 to 4 pounds, fat trimmed off*
2   *cloves garlic, quartered*
½   *teaspoon rosemary or fennel leaves*
      Salt and pepper
1   *cup sauterne wine*

> With sharp paring knife make deep slits in meat. Insert garlic and rosemary or fennel leaves. Rub outside of meat well with salt and pepper to taste.
>
> Place in roasting pan with wine. Roast uncovered in 350° oven until tender, allowing 40 minutes per pound. Baste meat as it roasts, adding more wine if needed.

SAUSAGES AND LENTILS

READY TRAY   Serves 4 to 6

1   *pound lentils, soaked overnight in water to cover*
2   *tablespoons olive oil*
1   *onion, finely chopped*
3   *tomatoes, peeled and coarsely chopped*
2   *sweet red peppers, seeded and coarsely chopped*
1   *large clove garlic, minced*
1   *pound small Italian sausages*
      Salt and freshly ground black pepper
2   *tablespoons parsley, finely chopped*

> Cook lentils in enough water to cover until tender.
>
> Sauté lightly in oil the onion, tomatoes, peppers and garlic.
>
> Add sausages, lentils, salt and pepper to taste and parsley. Cover and cook over low heat until sausages are cooked through and lentils are very soft.
>
> Serve with large pieces of crusty Italian bread.

In Italy this dish is usually served on New Year's day.

PORK CHOPS WITH FENNEL

Serves 4

2   cloves garlic
    Few fresh fennel leaves
4   tablespoons olive oil
    Salt and pepper
8   pork chops
    Celery leaf

Chop garlic and fennel leaves together until very fine. Add oil, salt and pepper to taste and blend thoroughly.
Dip the chops in the mixture, drain slightly and place on barbecue grill or under the broiler, and brown.
As chops cook, brush with a celery leaf dipped in the basting mixture.

SAUSAGES IN WINE

READY TRAY   Serves 4 to 6

2   pounds Italian sausage, sweet or hot
½   cup wine, red or white

Place sausages in shallow baking dish. Prick sausages with fork and pour in wine. Bake uncovered in 350° oven 30 minutes until golden brown. They may also be placed under the broiler, or cooked in a skillet on top of the stove.

PORK TENDERLOIN VICTOR

READY TRAY   Serves 2

4   pork tenderloins, ¼ inch thick
    Flour
4   teaspoons butter
⅓   cup seedless grapes
2   tablespoons Madeira wine
¼   cup fresh cream
½   teaspoon Worcestershire sauce
    Salt and freshly ground black pepper

Dust meat lightly with seasoned flour. Heat butter in heavy skillet, electric fry pan or crepe pan, and when it begins to bubble, add meat and brown on both sides well.

Remove meat, add grapes and wine and ignite. When flames burn out, add cream, Worcestershire sauce, salt and pepper to taste. Heat thoroughly and pour over browned meat before serving.

ROSEMARY SAUSAGE

READY TRAY

1	pound pork
1	pound beef
1	pound veal
1	pound suet
1	tablespoon salt
1	teaspoon freshly ground black pepper
2	teaspoons ground rosemary, or leaves chopped fine
½	teaspoon thyme
½	teaspoon marjoram
½	teaspoon freshly grated nutmeg
	Casings

Using the fine blade of the chopper, grind the pork, beef, veal and suet. Add remaining ingredients and mix well. Put into casings and tie every 4 inches, or form into patties, and refrigerate.

Variety Meats

The variety meats, besides providing some of our best sources of vitamins and minerals, make for very good eating.

Kidneys have a great affinity for wines. Veal and lamb kidneys are the most flavorful, and they cook very quickly. Beef kidney needs longer, slower cooking.

Calves' liver is at its best cooked quickly over high heat. Sweetbreads, which come from the neck or stomach regions of the animal, are a great delicacy; veal are the best. Brains also are very delicate and are often substituted in recipes that call for sweetbreads.

There are three types of tripe: honeycomb, which is the best, pocket and plain smooth. In itself tripe is flavorless, but a savory sauce turns it into an excellent dish.

Oxtails are on the bony side, but the meat is fine-flavored and the joints make an excellent stew.

Tongue—smoked, corned, pickled or canned—is good served hot or cold.

BRAINS IN CASSEROLE

READY TRAY   Serves 4

1   set veal or beef brains
4   tablespoons butter
1   tablespoon olive oil
    Salt and pepper
2   pinches allspice
2   egg yolks
2   tablespoons lemon juice

Parboil brains, clean and skin, being careful not to break.

Place butter and oil in warm casserole to melt. Place brains in casserole and spoon melted butter and oil over top. Salt and pepper to taste and sprinkle with allspice. Bake uncovered in 350° oven 45 minutes until tender. Remove to heated platter.

Blend egg yolks and lemon juice until smooth, add to casserole and cook until well blended. Pour over brains before serving.

91

CHICKEN LIVERS AND ANCHOVIES

Serves 4

4   green onions, finely chopped
2   teaspoons parsley, finely chopped
4   tablespoons butter
½   cup tomato sauce
1   pound chicken livers, cut in half
    Salt and pepper
4   anchovy fillets
2   egg yolks
1   tablespoon lemon juice

Sauté onions and parsley in butter over medium heat until wilted. Add tomato sauce and bring to boil. Add chicken livers, salt and pepper to taste. Use salt sparingly because anchovies are salty. Simmer until tender.

Add 2 tablespoons of sauce in which chicken livers are being cooked, to the anchovies, mashing thoroughly with a fork.

Beat egg yolks with lemon juice until very light and add anchovy mixture. Then add egg yolks to chicken livers, stirring gently until thoroughly blended.

CHICKEN LIVERS SAUTÉ

Serves 4

1½   pounds chicken livers, cut in half
½   cup diced prosciutto with fat
2   tablespoons onion, finely chopped
2   tablespoons green pepper, finely chopped
½   cup red wine
½   cup pitted ripe olives
1   tablespoon parsley, finely chopped
     Few leaves fresh thyme
     Toast

Sauté prosciutto, onion and peppers until meat is gently browned. Add chicken livers which have been lightly dusted in seasoned flour and sauté quickly on all sides.

Add wine, olives, parsley and thyme and simmer, stirring constantly until olives are heated.

Serve over toast.

VEAL KIDNEYS ROSSI

Serves 4

3   veal kidneys, fat removed, sliced very thin
4   tablespoons butter
½   cup fresh mushrooms, sliced
2   teaspoons shallots, finely chopped
½   cup brandy
½   cup sherry wine
½   teaspoon dry mustard
1   cup heavy cream
    Salt and freshly ground black pepper
    Trimmed triangles of toast, sautéed lightly in butter

Sauté the kidneys, mushrooms and shallots in butter until browned. Add brandy and wine, mustard, cream, and salt and pepper to taste. Heat thoroughly and serve over toast.

A pinch of rosemary leaves sprinkled over the kidneys while browning adds a special aroma and flavor.

KIDNEYS AND TOMATOES

Serves 4

1   pair kidneys, cut apart, fat removed
1   onion, finely chopped
3   tablespoons butter
2   tomatoes, peeled, seeded and chopped
    Salt and pepper
    Pinch fresh grated nutmeg
2   tablespoons broth
¼   cup red wine
    Flour
    Trimmed toast

Place kidneys in a large bowl and cover with boiling water. Let stand until water is cool. Drain and slice ¼ inch thick and set aside.

Sauté onion in 2 tablespoons butter until golden brown. Add tomatoes, salt and pepper to taste, nutmeg and broth. Simmer 10 minutes. Then add kidneys and wine. Blend remaining butter with 1 tablespoon flour. add to kidneys and simmer 5 minutes until sauce is smooth and slightly thickened.

Serve over toast.

CALVES' LIVER WITH WINE

Serves 4

1   *pound calves' liver, cut in 1-inch squares*
4   *tablespoons butter*
4   *tablespoons white wine*
1   *tablespoon flour*
     Salt and pepper

Sauté liver in butter over medium heat until browned. Blend wine and flour until smooth and pour over liver. Salt and pepper to taste and simmer 5 minutes, stirring until sauce is smooth.

OXTAIL STEW

Serves 6

3   *pounds oxtails, cut up and fat trimmed off*
1   *tablespoon olive oil*
1   *clove garlic, finely chopped*
2   *tablespoons flour*
     Salt
2   *whole cloves*
1   *bay leaf*
6   *peppercorns*
4   *cups water*
1   *cup red wine*
1   *cup whole-pack tomatoes*
12   *small white onions*
½   *cup sliced mushrooms*
4   *carrots, cut in 2-inch pieces*

Brown oxtails in hot oil in heavy kettle. Drain fat. Add garlic, flour, salt to taste, cloves, bay leaf and peppercorns. Stir until flour is thoroughly blended. Add water, wine and tomatoes. Cover and simmer slowly 3 hours until meat is tender and liquid is reduced to a thick sauce.

Add onions, mushrooms and carrots and cook until vegetables are tender, 30 minutes. Skim all excess fat before serving.

Serve chunks of crusty Italian bread with this for dunking in the sauce, which is one of the great treats of this tasty dish.

VEAL SWEETBREADS WITH MUSHROOMS

Serves 4

1   pound veal sweetbreads
6   large fresh mushrooms, quartered
2   tablespoons butter
2   tablespoons olive oil
1   onion, finely chopped
     Salt and pepper
¼   cup white wine
¼   cup broth
1   tablespoon flour
1   tablespoon butter
1   tablespoon parsley, finely chopped
     Pinch allspice
4   slices toast, trimmed and cut in triangles

Scald sweetbreads in salted boiling water. Remove outer thin membrane, clean thoroughly, removing connective tissues, and slice ¼ inch thick.

Sauté mushrooms and sweetbreads in butter and oil with onions until golden brown. Salt and pepper to taste, add wine and broth. Cover and simmer 30 minutes.

Add flour blended with 1 tablespoon butter to pan juices, with parsley and allspice. Simmer until thickened. Serve over toast.

VEAL SWEETBREADS AND FRESH PEAS

Serves 4

1   pound veal sweetbreads
1   onion, finely chopped
½   pound fresh mushrooms, quartered
4   tablespoons butter
2   tablespoons olive oil
½   pound fresh or frozen peas
     Salt and pepper
     Bay leaf
¼   cup broth

Scald sweetbreads in boiling water. Remove outer thin skin and clean thoroughly. Break into bite-size pieces.

Sauté sweetbreads, onions and mushrooms in butter and oil until golden brown.

Add peas, salt and pepper to taste, bay leaf and broth. Simmer 30 minutes until ingredients are tender, adding more broth if too dry.

TRIPE STEW

Serves 8

2   pounds tripe, well washed, cut in 1-inch pieces
2   tablespoons oil
1   onion, finely chopped
1   large green pepper, seeded and coarsely chopped
4   stalks celery, cut in ½-inch slices
1   pimiento, coarsely chopped
4   tomatoes, peeled and diced
2   bay leaves
    Pinch saffron
    Salt and pepper
1   cup broth
1   cup dry white wine

Sauté quickly in oil the onions, green pepper and celery. Add tripe, pimiento, tomatoes, bay leaves, saffron, salt and pepper to taste, broth and wine. Cover and simmer 2 to 3 hours until tender and sauce is reduced until thick.

This is good served over polenta or plain steamed rice.

TONGUE IN CASSEROLE

Serves 4 to 6

1   tongue (veal or beef)
4   tablespoons butter
1   onion, finely chopped
2   stalks celery, finely chopped
1   carrot, finely chopped
1   tablespoon parsley, finely chopped
12 large green olives, crushed gently
    Salt and pepper

Cover tongue with salted water and cook until tender, 2 to 3 hours. Remove outer skin, trim and place in casserole.

Sauté the onions, celery, carrot, parsley and olives in butter until golden brown. Add small amount of liquid in which the tongue was boiled to prevent dryness. Salt and pepper to taste, using salt sparingly because olives tend to be salty.

Pour sauce over tongue and bake uncovered in 350° oven 40 minutes, until meat is well permeated with sauce. Slice thin and serve with sauce.

CALVES' LIVER, ITALIAN STYLE

Serves 4

4   slices calves' liver, ½ inch thick
2   tablespoons butter
4   tablespoons shallots, finely chopped
2   tablespoons chives, finely chopped
1   tablespoon parsley, finely chopped
½   cup dry white wine
    Salt and freshly ground black pepper

Season liver with salt and pepper and sauté in butter quickly on both sides. Remove to hot plates.

Add shallots, chives and parsley to pan and sauté lightly. Add wine and simmer 3 minutes. Pour sauce over liver and serve immediately.

VEAL TONGUE PIQUANT

Serves 6 to 8

1   veal tongue
4   tablespoons olive oil
3   stalks celery, finely chopped
1   carrot, finely chopped
4   anchovy fillets, finely chopped
2   tablespoons pickled capers, finely chopped
1   green onion, finely chopped
1   slice bread, trimmed, dipped in vinegar and squeezed dry
    Juice of 1 whole lemon
    Salt and pepper

Cover tongue with salted water and boil until tender, 2 or 3 hours.

Heat oil and sauté celery and carrots 5 minutes.

Blend anchovies, capers, onions and bread until smooth and add to celery and carrots. Blend in lemon juice with few drops of oil, and add salt and pepper to taste.

When tongue is cooked and tender, remove outer skin, trim and slice thin.

Cover with sauce and marinate for several hours or overnight before serving.

VEAL BRAINS AND PROSCIUTTO

READY TRAY   Serves 4

 1 set veal brains
 1 onion, thinly sliced
 ¼ pound prosciutto, quartered
 2 tablespoons parsley, finely chopped
    Salt and pepper
 ¼ cup broth
 ¼ cup white wine
 4 tablespoons butter
 2 tablespoons flour
 6 tablespoons tomato sauce

Parboil brains 3 minutes. Clean, skin and slice ½ inch thick.

Place onion, prosciutto and 1 tablespoon parsley in saucepan. Place brains on top, salt and pepper to taste, add broth and wine, and simmer slowly 30 minutes.

Blend butter and flour thoroughly over low heat in separate saucepan until golden brown. Add tomato sauce, remainder of parsley and simmer 5 minutes. Pour sauce over brains before serving.

Cook it Outdoors

The ancient art of cooking over a bed of hot coals is practiced today by the man of the family when he shows off his skill over a barbecue grill in his backyard. One theory of the derivation of the word is itself entertaining: from whiskers, "barbe," to snout or tail, "cue," and gives one a vivid picture of a whole animal being skewered on a spit. In many parts of the world today whole animals are still being prepared in this way.

The recipes in this chapter suggest new ways to season those favorites of the barbecue—chicken and lamb—and other meats, which may become just as popular. You'll find it easier and more efficient to prepare the sauces and marinades ahead of time in the comfort of your own kitchen.

Barbecue grills come in all shapes and sizes, the most efficient having grates that may be raised or lowered so that the chef has some control of the heat. It's a good idea not to make the fire too large, since it is easier to add wood or briquettes to increase the bed of coals than it is to remove hot coals.

The grate should be greased before grilling foods and thoroughly cleaned when the barbecue is over so that the flavors of one delicious barbecue won't carry over to the next.

For a basting brush, tie together 3 stalks of celery with leaves, 3 sprigs fresh parsley and a generous sprig of fresh rosemary or marjoram. You will have not only a practical basting brush, but one that will add its own savory fragrance to the meat, fish or poultry that is going to be barbecued.

BARBECUED CHICKEN

READY TRAY   Serves 4

2	*whole broilers*
3	*cloves garlic, gently crushed*
	Fresh rosemary leaves
	Salt and pepper
¼	*cup white wine*
2	*tablespoons melted butter*
	Celery leaf for basting

99

Place one garlic clove, a few rosemary leaves and a little salt and pepper inside of each broiler. Truss, tie and place on spit lengthwise.

Blend wine, garlic, a few rosemary leaves, butter, salt and pepper to taste. Baste with celery leaf as broilers turn on spit.

Barbecue over hot coals 1 hour or more, depending on size.

BARBECUED BABY TURKEY

Serves 4 to 6

1   small turkey, 4 to 6 pounds ready-to-cook weight
    Salt and pepper
1   cup wine, white or red
2   tablespoons wine vinegar
½   cup olive oil
1   onion, grated
1   clove garlic, crushed
⅛   teaspoon thyme
⅛   teaspoon marjoram
⅛   teaspoon rosemary

Rub turkey thoroughly with salt and pepper, inside and out. Place on spit over charcoals.

Blend remaining ingredients and baste turkey as it turns on spit, until tender. Allow 20 minutes per pound, or longer, for desired tenderness.

BARBECUED FISH

Serves 6 to 8

1   large fish, cut in slices 1 inch thick, or
    small whole fish or fillets
    Salt and pepper
2   tablespoons melted butter or oil
½   cup wine, your choice
1   teaspoon herbs, your choice
    Juice of 1 lemon

Salt and pepper fish to taste on all sides. Blend butter, wine, herbs and lemon juice. Dip fish in sauce and place on grill skin side up, if split, and brown. Baste with sauce as fish barbecues. Then turn and continue cooking until done.

Serve with lemon wedges and garnish with parsley.

This is a simple way to prepare fish over very hot coals or in a hot oven. Be sure grids or broiler is well rubbed with oil or butter so fish does not stick when it is turned. Watch it carefully; if allowed to overcook, it will be dry.

Fish such as salmon, mackerel or trout need only be seasoned with salt and pepper and brushed with oil or butter before barbecuing or broiling.

BARBECUED KID

(CAPRETTO)

READY TRAY   Serves 6 to 8

1 kid
   Salt and pepper
3 cloves garlic, finely chopped
2 tablespoons butter
2 hot red chili peppers, finely chopped
1 onion, finely chopped
2 whole cloves
1 teaspoon marjoram
1 teaspoon sugar
2 tablespoons vinegar
1 cup white wine

Rub kid, left whole or split lengthwise, thoroughly with salt and pepper. Combine remaining ingredients and baste meat with sauce as it turns on spit.

If kid is oven-roasted, be sure first to sear meat on all sides in a hot oven (500°) for 20 minutes, then reduce heat to 350° and roast until tender. Allow 15 minutes per pound and baste from time to time with sauce.

When meat is tender, remove from roaster, skim all fat and pour sauce over carved meat.

BARBECUED LOIN OF LAMB

Serves 4 to 8

2   *loins of lamb, bones trimmed*
4   *tablespoons butter, melted*
2   *tablespoons olive oil*
2   *cloves garlic, crushed*
2   *teaspoons rosemary leaves*
    Salt and pepper

> Start charcoal fire at least 30 minutes before you are ready to barbecue. Place meat on spit.
> Blend butter, oil, garlic, rosemary, salt and pepper to taste. Baste meat with sauce as it cooks until medium done. Before serving, remove bone from each loin and slice meat in thick pieces.

BARBECUED VEAL SWEETBREADS

READY TRAY   Serves 4 to 6

2   *pounds veal sweetbreads*
1   *pound large fresh mushrooms, cut in half*
2   *tablespoons melted butter*
1   *tablespoon lemon juice*
2   *tablespoons white wine*
    Fresh rosemary leaves
    Salt and pepper
    Celery leaf for basting

> Scald sweetbreads in boiling water 5 minutes. Remove outer thin skin and clean thoroughly. Cut in 1-inch pieces.
> Alternate mushrooms and sweetbreads on skewers until used up.
> Blend thoroughly butter, lemon juice, wine, rosemary leaves, and salt and pepper to taste, and baste with celery leaf until tender, approximately 20 minutes.

> The veal sweetbreads and mushrooms can be broiled, if desired, in hot oven.

BARBECUED VEAL WITH MUSHROOMS

Serves 4

2   pounds veal shoulder, cut in 1½-inch cubes
    Bay leaves
1   pound large fresh mushrooms
2   green bell peppers, cut in 1½-inch squares
½   cup dry white wine
2   cloves garlic, finely chopped
2   tablespoons olive oil
    Salt and pepper
    Celery leaf for basting

> Any part of the veal may be used, but the shoulder has more flavor than other cuts.
>
> Alternate on skewers the veal, bay leaves, mushrooms and bell pepper. Continue until all ingredients are used.
>
> Blend wine, garlic, oil, salt and pepper to taste. Baste veal with celery leaf or basting brush until tender.

BARBECUED VEAL

Serves 6

3   pounds loin or rump of veal, cut in one thick piece
3   tablespoons olive oil
½   cup red wine
1   teaspoon fresh rosemary, finely chopped
    Salt and pepper
    Celery leaf for basting

> Roll veal and tie tightly 1 inch apart with heavy cord, forming a cylinder, and place on spit lengthwise over hot coals.
>
> Blend oil, wine, rosemary, salt and pepper to taste. Using celery leaf, baste meat as it cooks.
>
> Test with a large barbecue fork for tenderness. It is done when fork penetrates to the center without forcing. It should be ready to serve in about 1 hour.
>
> The sliced veal may be served plain or with a prepared salsa of your choice.

BARBECUED PORK LIVER IN CAUL FAT

Serves 6 to 8

2   *pounds pork liver, ½ inch thick, cut in 1½-inch squares*
    Salt and pepper
    Caul fat or fat back, cut in thin strips
    Bay leaves
    Stale bread, cut in 1½-inch squares
    Oil
    Butter

Season liver with salt and pepper to taste. Wrap each piece with strip of fat. Place on spit, alternating with bay leaf, bread and fat-wrapped meat.

Barbecue until medium well; beyond this stage, the liver tends to toughen.

Baste with oil and butter or salsa of your choice.

(Caul fat is the netlike membrane covering the heart and intestines of the animal. Pork caul fat is the best.)

BARBECUED SKEWERED LAMB

READY TRAY   Serves 4 to 6

2   *pounds ground lamb shoulder*
2   *cloves garlic, finely chopped*
2   *eggs*
1   *cup pine nuts*
½   *cup parsley, finely chopped*
½   *teaspoon mint leaves, finely chopped*
    Salt and pepper
    Oil

Combine ingredients thoroughly. Mold around skewers in oblong shape 1 inch thick and 6 inches long. Brush with oil.

Barbecue over hot coals, approximately 15 minutes, basting with oil while cooking. Slip off skewers before serving.

These lamb rolls can also be broiled.

BARBECUED PORK FILLET

Serves 6 to 8

2   pounds pork fillet, cut in 1-inch cubes
    Stale bread, trimmed and cut in 1-inch cubes
1   pound prosciutto, cut in 1-inch cubes
    Bay leaves
    Salt and pepper

>   Alternate on skewers in following order—bread, bay
>   leaf, prosciutto and pork—until all ingredients are used,
>   ending each skewer with a piece of bread. Salt and
>   pepper to taste.
>   Barbecue 1 hour or longer. Serve plain or with a pre-
>   pared salsa, which may also be used to baste the meat
>   as it cooks.

BARBECUED LAMB WITH PROSCIUTTO

READY TRAY   Serves 4

2   pounds lamb shoulder or leg, boned and cut in 1½-inch cubes
    Salt and pepper
    Stale bread, trimmed and cut in 1½-inch squares
1   pound prosciutto, ½ inch thick, cut in 1½-inch squares
    Sprigs of fresh sage
    Melted butter
    Olive oil

>   Season meat to taste with salt and pepper.
>   Alternate on skewers—bread, sage leaf, lamb and pros-
>   ciutto—until all ingredients are used.
>   Place over hot charcoal fire and baste with melted
>   butter and oil until medium done.

BARBECUED FRESH VEGETABLES

GRILLED ONIONS

Peel large sweet onions and cut in slices 1 inch thick. Dip in melted
butter and arrange in a long-handled double broiler. Cook quickly

over hot coals until golden brown on both sides. Season to taste with salt and freshly ground black pepper before serving.

ROASTED FRESH CORN

Turn back the husks of freshly picked corn without removing them, pull out and discard the silks, dip ears in cold water and pull up husks to cover the ears.

Lay ears of corn on grill over hot coals and roast, turning frequently, about 20 minutes. Serve with butter, salt and freshly ground black pepper.

BROILED EGGPLANT

Peel large eggplant and cut into ½-inch slices. Marinate for an hour in garlic-seasoned olive oil. Arrange slices in long-handled double broiler and cook over hot coals until golden brown on both sides.

BROILED TOMATOES

Cut firm tomatoes in half, brush with butter and sprinkle with finely chopped basil and fine breadcrumbs. Place in long-handled double broiler and cook over coals until lightly browned. Season to taste with salt and pepper when serving.

CUCUMBER AND MUSHROOMS

Peel large firm cucumbers and cut in slices 1-inch thick. Arrange on skewers alternately with large mushroom caps. Dip in melted butter and cook over hot coals, 10 minutes.

Brush with more melted butter and sprinkle with pepper before serving.

BARBECUED FRESH FRUITS

BARBECUED BANANAS

Choose firm, slightly green bananas. Leave the skins on and lay them on the grates over the coals. Cook about 15 minutes, turning carefully with a pair of tongs or two spoons when half-cooked.

Serve in skins. To eat, strip off a section of the peel and scoop soft pulp out with a spoon.

PINEAPPLE

Cut whole unpeeled pineapple into 6 wedges. Cut away woody core and sprinkle with dark rum. Place wedges, skin side down directly on the grill over the coals, and cook until heated through and softened. Serve immediately.

Poultry

References to chicken are said to have been found in Chinese writing of 1400 B.C., and there must be as many ways for preparing chicken as the years that have passed since that date!

Here are a few ways to prepare it in the Italian style. Chicken cacciatore in its own tomato sauce, for example, but how about a different flavor like chicken with fennel or with green olives? Or for a change you might try a roast duck or goose with a chestnut-sausage stuffing that is different and delicious.

CHICKEN IN CASSEROLE

READY TRAY   Serves 4

1   *whole roasting chicken, ready to cook*
    Giblets
2   *green onions, sliced thin*
1   *stalk celery, finely chopped*
2   *tablespoons butter*
2   *tablespoons parsley, finely chopped*
4   *dried mushrooms, soaked and chopped*
2   *slices prosciutto, minced*
1   *egg, lightly beaten*
2   *tablespoons grated Parmesan cheese*
    Salt and pepper
    Breadcrumbs
    Oil

Parboil giblets 10 minutes and chop fine.

Brown onions and celery in butter. Add parsley, mushrooms, giblets and prosciutto; heat thoroughly. Remove from heat and blend in egg, cheese, salt and pepper to taste. Add enough breadcrumbs to hold together. Stuff bird lightly with this dressing and secure opening.

Brush chicken evenly with oil, place in casserole and roast uncovered in 350° oven for 30 minutes. Cover casserole and continue roasting until tender.

108

CHICKEN WITH FENNEL

Serves 4

1   broiler
2   thin slices prosciutto, minced
2   cloves garlic
¼   head fennel, cut in strips lengthwise
4   peppercorns
2   tablespoons olive oil
      Salt and pepper

> Stuff broiler with the prosciutto, garlic, fennel and peppercorns.
>
> Truss broiler and tie legs. Brush skin with oil and sprinkle with salt and pepper to taste.
>
> Place in casserole or roaster and roast uncovered in 400° oven until browned, 25 minutes. Reduce heat to 325°, cover casserole and roast until tender, 35 to 45 minutes.

CHICKEN CACCIATORE

Serves 4 to 6

1   large fryer, cut in serving pieces
      Salt and pepper
      Flour
¼   cup olive oil
1   large clove garlic, finely chopped
12   whole small white onions, peeled
2   green bell peppers, seeded and cut in 1-inch pieces
2   cups whole-pack tomatoes, juice strained
1   pimiento, chopped
½   cup white wine
½   teaspoon oregano
1   cup sliced mushrooms

> Dust chicken pieces lightly with seasoned flour.
>
> In a large heavy skillet, brown chicken quickly on all sides in oil. Add garlic, onions and green pepper and brown quickly. Add tomatoes, pimiento, wine and ore-

gano. Cover and simmer until tender, 45 minutes. Add sliced mushrooms and simmer 20 minutes until tender and sauce is reduced.

Serve with plain risotto, polenta or your favorite pasta, and a green tossed salad.

CHICKEN FRA DIAVOLO

When a dish is described as being "fra diavolo," it means that it is going to be a hot, spicy one due to the chili peppers used in its preparation—in other words, as Brother Devil would prepare it for his fellow devils!

READY TRAY   Serves 4

1   chicken, cut in serving pieces
4   tablespoons butter
2   tablespoons olive oil
4   green onions, sliced ½ inch thick
1   clove garlic, mashed
     Salt
⅓   cup red wine
2   small red chili peppers, crushed fine
½   cup tomato sauce

Heat butter and oil in heavy skillet and brown chicken pieces evenly. Add onion, garlic and salt to taste. When browned, add wine and chili peppers. When wine is almost absorbed, add tomato sauce and blend well.

Cover and simmer 45 minutes to 1 hour, until tender.

CHICKEN BREAST TARRAGON

READY TRAY   Serves 4 to 6

3   chicken breasts, boned and cut in half
4   tablespoons butter
6   shallots, finely chopped
½   cup apricot or peach brandy
2   egg yolks, lightly beaten
1   cup light cream
2   tablespoons fresh tarragon leaves, finely chopped
     Salt and freshly ground black pepper

110

Over low heat sauté the flattened chicken breasts gently in butter, seasoning with salt and freshly ground black pepper to taste. When tender, place on a heated serving platter.

Add shallots to butter in pan and sauté until glossy. Add 2 tablespoons brandy and deglaze the pan. Gradually blend in egg yolks beaten with cream and stir until thickened. Remove from heat and add tarragon leaves.

Pour remainder of brandy over chicken breasts. Ignite, and when burned out, cover quickly with sauce and serve.

CHICKEN CUTLETS

READY TRAY   Serves 4

2   chicken breasts, boned and cut in half
1   egg, lightly beaten
1   teaspoon parsley, finely chopped
    Salt and pepper
    Breadcrumbs
4   tablespoons butter
1   tablespoon olive oil
¼   cup white wine

Pound each breast of chicken flat with the broad side of a heavy knife.

Blend egg, parsley, salt and pepper to taste, and dip chicken cutlets in mixture. Then dip in breadcrumbs, patting smooth on both sides.

Sauté the cutlets over low heat in butter and oil, turning often until nicely browned. Add wine and simmer 5 minutes.

CHICKEN WITH GREEN OLIVES

READY TRAY   Serves 4

1   broiler, 3½ pounds, cut into serving pieces
4   tablespoons butter
12 large green olives, pitted and quartered
½   cup tomato sauce
    Salt and pepper

111

Brown chicken pieces in butter on all sides. Add olives and brown lightly. Add tomato sauce, with salt and pepper to taste. Cover and simmer until tender, adding more tomato sauce, broth or water if it becomes too dry.

It is said that a taste for olives must be cultivated. In this recipe the addition of olives gives the dish a slightly sour but piquant taste all its own.

ROAST GOOSE WITH CHESTNUT DRESSING

READY TRAY   Serves 6 to 10

4   pounds fresh Italian chestnuts
4   tablespoons butter
½   pound Italian bulk sausage
1   tablespoon parsley, finely chopped
1   clove garlic, finely chopped
*   Goose liver, scalded and finely chopped*
1   goose, 10 to 12 pounds, ready to cook
*   Salt and pepper*
*   White wine*
*   Watercress*

With sharp knife slit shells of 2 pounds of chestnuts on convex side. Cover chestnuts with water and bring to a boil. While still hot, remove shells and inner skins from chestnuts and chop.

Sauté chestnuts with butter, sausage, parsley and garlic over low heat for 10 minutes, breaking up sausage with fork. Add chopped goose liver and cook for 10 minutes.

Wipe goose with damp cloth and stuff with dressing. Close opening. Rub outside of goose with 1 tablespoon salt. Turn skin of neck backward and secure with small skewer. Twist wings back and tie legs. Prick bird with fork to let fats escape. Place on rack in roaster and roast uncovered in 375° oven until tender, allowing 20 minutes per pound. Prick with fork occasionally during roasting period. When bird is tender, drain all fat from roasting pan.

Remove shells and skins from balance of chestnuts, cover with white wine, salt and pepper to taste, and simmer over low heat 30 minutes.

Garnish roasted goose with whole chestnuts and watercress.

CHICKEN WITH EGG NOODLES

Serves 4 to 6

1   *broiler, cut in serving pieces*
4   *green onions*
1   *carrot, cut in half lengthwise*
4   *sprigs parsley*
1   *stalk celery, cut in 4-inch pieces*
2   *sprigs fresh basil*
    Salt and pepper
4   *tablespoons butter*
2   *tablespoons flour*
12 *ounces egg noodles*
2   *tablespoons grated Parmesan cheese*

Tie all vegetables together in a bunch and place in kettle with the chicken and seasoning and hot water to cover. Cover kettle, bring to a boil, skimming foam as it forms. Add salt and pepper to taste, reduce heat and simmer until tender.

Remove vegetables and chicken, and strain broth. Blend butter with flour and add to broth, stirring until sauce is thick and smooth.

Cook noodles in boiling water and drain. Add a small amount of chicken gravy and turn into a casserole. Sprinkle with cheese and bake uncovered in 350° oven 10 minutes.

Serve with chicken and thickened sauce.

ROAST DUCK OR GOOSE

Serves 4 to 6

1   *duck or goose, ready to cook*
4   *tablespoons olive oil*
    Salt and pepper
1   *onion, finely chopped*
2   *stalks celery, finely chopped*
3   *bay leaves, broken in small pieces*
¼   *cup white wine*
1   *cup broth*
2   *tablespoons butter*
2   *tablespoons flour*

Rub duck or goose well with oil, and salt and pepper to taste. Place in roasting pan and pour over remainder of oil. Sprinkle with onion, celery and bay leaves.

Roast uncovered in 375° oven until it begins to brown. Pour over wine, cover roasting pan, reduce heat to 325° and continue roasting until bird is tender, basting with pan juices from time to time.

When done, remove bird and keep warm. Strain liquid in roasting pan and add wine and broth or water to make 2 cups. Bring to a boil and slowly stir in butter blended with flour, until sauce is thick and smooth. Correct seasonings before serving over carved fowl.

TURKEY BREAST FONTINA

READY TRAY   Serves 4

1   turkey breast, skinned and cut into 4 fillets
    Salt and pepper
    Flour
2   tablespoons butter
¼   cup sauterne wine
2   tablespoons Marsala wine
4   thin slices fontina cheese

Flatten turkey meat with broad side of a heavy knife. Salt and pepper to taste and flour lightly.

Sauté in butter 10 minutes. Add wines and heat thoroughly. Place cheese over turkey fillets, cover skillet and allow cheese to melt before serving.

ROAST CAPON

READY TRAY   Serves 4 to 6

1   whole capon
4   thin slices prosciutto
2   thin slices salt pork
1   stalk celery, cut in ½-inch pieces
1   carrot, cut in ½-inch pieces
¼   cup white wine
½   cup broth
    Salt and pepper
6   fresh mushrooms, sliced

114

Wrap slices of prosciutto around the capon, making sure the breast is well covered, and place in roasting pan on top of salt pork slices. Add celery, carrot, wine and broth to roasting pan, with salt and pepper to taste. Roast uncovered in 350° oven, until done.

Remove capon carefully from pan and keep hot, discarding salt pork. Chop prosciutto very fine, and strain liquid from roasting pan. Add mushrooms and chopped prosciutto to the strained liquid and simmer 10 minutes. Serve as sauce with carved capon.

SKILLET CHICKEN OR CAPON

READY TRAY   Serves 4

1   chicken or capon, cut into serving pieces
     Salt and pepper
4   tablespoons butter
2   tablespoons olive oil
1   onion, coarsely chopped
1   carrot, cut in 1-inch pieces
¼   cup white wine
4   dried mushrooms, soaked, drained and chopped
1   tablespoon tomato paste, diluted with 3 tablespoons water
                        or
4   tablespoons tomato sauce

Salt and pepper chicken pieces to taste and brown on all sides in heavy skillet in butter and oil. Add onions and carrot, and when onions are wilted, add wine. When wine is absorbed, add the mushrooms and tomato sauce.

Cover and simmer until tender, stirring occasionally. Add a little broth or hot water if it becomes too dry.

115

Game

The Italians use a lot of game prepared in many ways, especially small birds of all kinds, which are not available here due to our game law restrictions.

When some well-meaning friend bestows upon you some of the game he has enjoyed hunting and you ask yourself, "What do I do now?" here is a handful of recipes that are enjoyable and tasty. Don't wait for a friend to go duck-hunting in order to try the recipe for Wild Duck, fifteenth-century style. Get a duck from your local market and you'll have roast duck stuffed with rice in a delicious orange sauce.

RABBIT PIQUANT

READY TRAY   Serves 4 to 6

1   *rabbit fryer, cut in serving pieces*
    Salt and pepper
    Flour
¼   *pound butter*
2   *tablespoons olive oil*
1   *onion, finely chopped*
1   *carrot, finely chopped*
2   *stalks celery, finely chopped*
3   *dried mushrooms, soaked, drained and chopped*
4   *whole cloves*
2   *pinches allspice*
½   *cup red wine*
½   *cup broth*
2   *tablespoons pickled capers*
3   *anchovy fillets, finely mashed*
1   *tablespoon parsley, finely chopped*

Salt and pepper rabbit pieces lightly and flour. Sauté in butter and oil 10 minutes. Add onions, carrot, celery, mushrooms, cloves and allspice. When onions are wilted, add wine and broth, cover and simmer 20 minutes.

Remove meat and force sauce through a strainer. Replace sauce and rabbit in pan, add capers, anchovies and parsley and simmer until tender.

116

VENISON STEW

Serves 4 to 6

3   pounds venison, cut in 1½-inch squares
1   onion, coarsely chopped
3   cloves garlic, crushed
6   sprigs parsley
2   sprigs fresh rosemary
4   bay leaves
6   whole cloves
1   cup red wine
¼   cup vinegar
¼   pound butter
    Salt and pepper
1   No. 2½ can tomatoes, drained and chopped, juice reserved

Place in a large bowl in alternating layers the meat and then onion, garlic, parsley, rosemary, bay leaves and cloves. Add wine and vinegar, cover bowl and marinate 48 hours. If liquid does not cover the meat, add more wine and vinegar in 4-to-1 ratio. Drain meat well and reserve marinade.

Salt and pepper to taste and braise meat thoroughly in butter. Add tomatoes and simmer, covered, until tender. Blend juice from tomatoes with 1 cup of marinade and add to meat, a small amount at a time as it cooks. Serve with polenta.

The venison may be left in one whole piece and marinated. Roast covered in moderate oven (350°) until tender, but omit chopped tomatoes. Baste with tomato juice blended with the marinade.

VENISON CHOPS OR CUTLETS

Serves 4

8   venison chops or cutlets, ½ inch thick
    Salt and pepper
    Flour
¼   pound butter
½   cup red wine
2   tablespoons jelly, your choice

Flatten and smooth chops or cutlets with the broad side of a heavy knife to tenderize. Salt and pepper to taste and flour lightly.

Sauté in butter until medium rare. Remove meat and keep hot.

Add wine and jelly to pan juices and when jelly is melted, pour over venison before serving.

WILD DUCK FIFTEENTH CENTURY

READY TRAY   Serves 2

      2 wild ducks, ready to cook
         Giblets, finely chopped
  1¼ cups orange juice
    ¼ cup brandy
      1 cup wild rice
      4 cups water
      1 cup chicken broth
      4 tablespoons sweet butter, softened
      1 tablespoon chives, finely chopped
      1 tablespoon green onions, finely chopped
      1 tablespoon celery leaves, finely chopped
      1 tablespoon fresh basil, finely chopped
      1 tablespoon gin
         Salt and freshly ground black pepper
         Pinch of fresh grated nutmeg
      1 teaspoon grated orange rind
      2 teaspoons lemon juice
      2 cups dry red wine
      3 tablespoons curaçao

Rub outside and inside of ducks thoroughly with ¼ cup of orange juice with brandy, and set aside.

Add rice slowly to boiling water with 1 teaspoon salt and cook 4 minutes. Reduce heat, add chicken broth, cover tightly and simmer 30 to 45 minutes until rice is tender.

Cream butter in saucepan with chives, onions, celery leaves and basil. Blend in gin, salt and pepper to taste and nutmeg. Add drained rice and giblets, mix thoroughly and cook 5 minutes. Stuff ducks with rice mixture and place in roaster.

Blend together 1 cup orange juice, orange rind, lemon juice and 1 cup wine and pour over ducks. Roast uncovered in 400° oven 15 to 25 minutes depending on

118

age and size of ducks. Baste often with sauce. When ducks are roasted to desired doneness, generally on the rare side, remove to hot serving platter.

Add remainder of wine and curaçao to pan juices, scraping pan well. Bring liquid to boil, and pour over ducks before serving. Serve sauce with carved duck and wild rice.

ROAST WILD DUCK

READY TRAY   Serves 2

2   *wild ducks, ready to cook*
4   *stalks celery, cut in 2-inch pieces*
4   *tablespoons olive oil*
    Salt and pepper

Rub outside of each duck well with oil. Place celery pieces inside of each duck, and salt and pepper to taste inside and out.

Roast in hot oven, 400°, 10 to 15 minutes.

Serve 1 whole duck per person.

PHEASANT DE BENEDETTI

READY TRAY   Serves 4

1   *pheasant*
    Butter
1   *shallot, minced*
    Brandy
    Cognac

Breast and disjoint pheasant at hip, and skin. Place a generous amount of butter and a minced shallot in two fry pans. Heat one pan to bubbly, add legs and cook over medium heat until brown, 8 or 9 minutes. Sprinkle with brandy, cover and keep over very low heat.

Five minutes after starting legs, heat second pan and add breasts. Brown, turn and cook until milky all the way through. Add legs and flame with Cognac. Do not cook further: it will toughen and require an hour or more to become tender again.

119

Sauce No. 1

Brown sixteen walnut halves in butter. Add 1 cup apricot-pineapple preserves, juice of a fresh orange, 1 jigger cointreau and ½ cup port wine. Heat, and serve in sauce boat.

Sauce No. 2

Heat together 1 cup lingonberry preserves, 1 jigger Crème de Cassis and ½ cup port wine. Serve in sauce boat.

Serve with wild rice or with hominy grits sliced and browned in butter.

fish

The abundance and varieties of fresh fish in Italy have produced many delectable ways of preparing it. There's a tasty way to cook every kind of fish that comes your way. You can broil, sauté, poach, boil or bake it; or you can make a fish stew, a *cioppino*, from several varieties.

Just keep in mind that fish should not be overcooked. It is ready to serve when the flesh has lost its translucent appearance and flakes easily.

BASS WITH OLIVES

READY TRAY   Serves 4 to 6

 1 *whole bass, 3 to 4 pounds, scaled and cleaned*
 4 *tablespoons butter*
 1 *onion, chopped*
 1 *clove garlic, finely chopped*
 2 *tablespoons parsley, finely chopped*
 4 *fresh mushrooms, sliced*
 2 *cups whole-pack tomatoes, chopped*
 1 *cup clam juice*
 ½ *teaspoon oregano*
    Salt and pepper
12 *green olives stuffed with pimiento, sliced*
 1 *pimiento, cut in narrow strips*
    Watercress

Place fish in large roaster.

To prepare sauce: Brown onion, garlic and parsley in butter. Add mushrooms, tomatoes, clam juice, oregano, salt and pepper to taste. Simmer 30 minutes. Add olives and pour sauce over fish. Bake uncovered in 375° oven 35 minutes until fish is tender and flaky. Baste with sauce during baking period.

Serve whole with pimiento strips over the top, and garnish with watercress.

121

ABALONE

Serves 2 to 4

2   *large abalone steaks, 1/4 inch thick, tenderized and cut in half*
    Salt and pepper
    Flour
2   *eggs, lightly beaten*
1/4 *cup olive oil*
1/4 *cup sweet butter*
    Juice of 1 lemon
1   *tablespoon chopped parsley*
    Lemon wedges

Salt and pepper abalone steaks to taste. Flour lightly, dip in egg, then flour and then egg. Brown on both sides quickly in very hot oil and butter, allowing not more than 1 minute for complete cooking time, since overcooking will make them tough.

Remove fish, add lemon juice and parsley to pan. Heat thoroughly for 1 minute, stirring, and pour over fish.

Serve with lemon wedges.

BAKED CLAMS

Serves 2

12 *clams*
    Salt and pepper
1   *tablespoon scallions, finely chopped*
4   *tablespoons breadcrumbs*
2   *tablespoons grated Parmesan cheese*
    Juice of 1 lemon
2   *tablespoons melted butter*
1/3 *cup sherry wine*
    Paprika

Open and leave clam in one half shell. Reserve juice. Place clams in shallow baking dish. Pour small amount of clam juice over each clam. Salt and pepper to taste, and sprinkle with scallions.

Mix breadcrumbs and cheese together and sprinkle lightly over each clam.

Pour a little lemon juice over each one, then melted butter. Add wine around edges of each clam shell.

122

Sprinkle lightly with paprika and bake uncovered in 400° oven 20 minutes until browned.

BAKED CLAMS OREGANO

Serves 4

2   cloves garlic
4   sprigs fresh parsley
1   teaspoon fresh oregano (if available), or dried oregano
½   cup breadcrumbs
½   cup butter, softened
    Salt and pepper
24 cherrystone clams, on the half shell
    Rock salt

Chop garlic, parsley and oregano together very fine. Add breadcrumbs, softened butter and salt and pepper to taste. Blend until very smooth. Spread 1 tablespoon of mixture over each half clam.

Spread rock salt in thick layer over the bottom of a baking dish. Set clams on this bed of salt and bake uncovered in 475° oven about 10 minutes, or until the edges of the clams begin to curl. Do not overbake.

PAPA ROSSI'S STEAMED CLAMS

Serves 2

2   dozen clams in shells
2   tablespoons olive oil
2   cloves garlic, finely chopped
1   tablespoon parsley, finely chopped
1   tablespoon fresh sweet basil, finely chopped
2   tablespoons melted butter

When purchasing clams, be sure they are tightly closed to insure absolute freshness. Scrub clam shells thoroughly under running cool water. Place in large kettle with water to cover, and let stand for at least 2 hours, to get rid of sand. Drain clams.

Heat oil and sauté garlic until golden brown. Add drained clams. More water need not be added, since the clams will have retained enough liquid for the broth. However, more water may be added if so desired, but the broth will not be as concentrated and pungent. Sprinkle with parsley and basil. Cover tightly and allow to steam over medium heat, 15 to 20 minutes, until clam shells are partially opened.

Serve 12 clams per person in a shallow soup plate. Blend butter with strained clam broth and serve separately as a dip.

CRAB LEGS FLORENTINE

READY TRAY   Serves 2

1   *pound crab legs*
    Salt and pepper
1   *teaspoon grated onion*
1   *teaspoon parsley, finely chopped*
2   *tablespoons melted butter*
½   *cup chopped cooked spinach*
½   *cup breadcrumbs*

Place crab legs in shallow baking dish, meat side up. Salt and pepper to taste.

Combine onion, parsley and 1 tablespoon melted butter and spread over crab legs. Spread chopped spinach over top and sprinkle with breadcrumbs. Pour 1 tablespoon butter over all.

Bake uncovered in 400° oven 20 minutes until top is lightly browned.

CRAB LEGS DIABLE

READY TRAY   Serves 4

24 *crab legs, shelled*
    Flour
2   *eggs, lightly beaten*
¼   *pound butter*
4   *tablespoons A-1 sauce*
2   *teaspoons dry mustard*
¼   *cup pale dry sherry wine*
2   *tablespoons Cognac or brandy*
    Salt and pepper
2   *cups steamed wild rice*

124

Press crab legs gently in flour, then dip in beaten egg. Sauté in 4 tablespoons butter until golden brown, season with salt and pepper to taste. Set aside and keep warm.

Blend 4 tablespoons butter, A-1 sauce and mustard until smooth. Season with freshly ground black pepper to taste. Place sautéed crab legs in sauce and heat gently. Add wine and pour Cognac or brandy around outer edges of pan. Pull pan toward you so the fumes from the Cognac may be ignited, if so desired.

Serve over steamed wild rice.

CIOPPINO SAN FRANCISCO

Cioppino simply means chopped. This recipe is for a fish stew, Italian style, which is said to have originated in Genoa. However, it is the fishermen of the San Francisco area who can really claim this wonderfully tasty dish as their own, using this method of preparing their catches of crab and other fresh fish.

READY TRAY   Serves 6 to 8

1   onion, sliced
1   bunch green onions, sliced
1   green pepper, seeded and diced
2   cloves garlic, minced
¼   cup olive oil
2   tablespoons chopped parsley
1   cup tomato puree
1   cup tomato sauce
1   cup white or red wine
1   cup water
1   bay leaf
     Salt and pepper
¼   teaspoon rosemary leaves
¼   teaspoon thyme
2   live crabs, cleaned and cracked
12   fresh clams in shells
1   pound fresh shrimp in shells

Split crabs with cleaver, wash and clean under running water. Remove claws and divide at the joints and crack with mallet. Cut and crack crab in serving pieces, with the shells.

Sauté onion, green onions, green pepper and garlic in oil five minutes. Add parsley, tomato puree, tomato

125

sauce, wine, water, bay leaf, salt and pepper to taste, rosemary and thyme. Cover and simmer slowly 1 hour.

Place cracked crab pieces on the bottom of a large kettle. Place clams and shrimp over crab. Pour hot sauce over, cover and simmer slowly 30 minutes until clam shells begin to open.

LOBSTER TAILS

READY TRAY   Serves 6

6   large lobster tails
    Salt and pepper
    Flour
2   eggs, lightly beaten
½   cup milk
4   tablespoons olive oil
2   tablespoons butter
2   tablespoons shallots, finely chopped
6   large fresh mushrooms, sliced
2   green onions, chopped
¼   cup sherry wine
1   tablespoon parsley, finely chopped

Cut lobster tails lengthwise through top shell. Remove meat, clean, wash and drain thoroughly. Salt and pepper to taste.

Roll in flour lightly and dip in beaten egg blended with milk. Sauté in hot oil until golden brown on both sides. Drain off all oil. Add butter, shallots, mushrooms and green onions to pan. Sauté until wilted. Add wine and parsley, and cook 5 to 8 minutes before serving.

SAUTÉED OCTOPUS

READY TRAY   Serves 4 to 6

1   octopus, 2 pounds
    Flour
½   cup olive oil
    Salt and pepper
    Lemon wedges

126

Octopus tastes much like abalone steak when sautéed.
Clean, tenderize and skin the octopus. Cut tentacles in
2-inch lengths, and cut body into strips 1 by 2 inches.
Flour lightly. Sauté in oil quickly until golden brown.
Salt and pepper to taste after it is sautéed.
Serve with lemon wedges.

BAKED OYSTERS ITALIAN

READY TRAY   Serves 4 to 6

2   dozen oysters on the half shell
1   small onion, minced
1   stalk celery, minced
1   tablespoon fresh watercress, minced
½   cup melted butter
¾   cup breadcrumbs
4   tablespoons grated Parmesan cheese
    Salt and pepper
    Pinch ground anise
    Rock salt

Combine all ingredients thoroughly, except the oysters
and rock salt. Pour thick layer of rock salt on the bottom
of a baking dish, and sprinkle with a little water, just
enough to dampen.

Pour liquid off oysters. Spoon 1 tablespoon of the
blended mixture on each oyster in the half shell. Arrange shells on bed of salt and bake uncovered in 450°
oven 5 to 8 minutes until top of oysters is lightly
browned.

SCALLOPS MARINARA

READY TRAY   Serves 4

1   pound scallops, cut in serving pieces
2   tablespoons olive oil
1   clove garlic, finely chopped
    Pinch red pepper
1   teaspoon chopped parsley
⅓   cup white wine
1   tomato, peeled and chopped
    Salt and pepper

Sauté garlic in oil until golden brown. Add red pepper, parsley and scallops, stirring for several minutes until browned evenly on all sides. Add wine, cover and simmer 5 minutes. Add tomato, salt and pepper to taste, and cook 10 minutes.

Serve with own sauce.

PAN-FRIED SCALLOPS

READY TRAY   Serves 4

  2 *pounds scallops*
     Breadcrumbs
 ½   *cup butter or olive oil*
 ⅓   *cup white wine*
     Salt and pepper
     Lemon wedges

Salt and pepper the scallops to taste, and roll lightly in breadcrumbs to coat.

Sauté in butter or oil until golden brown on all sides.

Add wine to butter in pan and cook 2 minutes. Pour over scallops before serving. Serve with lemon wedges.

SCALLOPS CACCIATORE

READY TRAY   Serves 4

  1 *pound scallops*
 ¼   *cup olive oil*
  1 *large green pepper, seeded and cut in ½-inch squares*
 ½   *pound fresh mushrooms, sliced*
  1 *onion, finely chopped*
  1 *clove garlic, finely chopped*
  2 *cups whole-pack tomatoes, strained and chopped*
     Salt and pepper
 ⅓   *cup white wine*

Brown scallops in oil and set aside.

In same pan sauté pepper, mushrooms, onions and garlic until wilted. Add tomatoes, salt and pepper to taste, and bring to boil slowly. Reduce heat and simmer 30 minutes until tomatoes are well cooked. Add scallops

and wine. Heat thoroughly. Sauce may be thickened with flour or cornstarch mixed with a little cold water.
Serve over cooked spaghetti or noodles.

SQUID

1½   *pounds squid, 6 to 8 inches long*
     Flour
¼   *cup olive oil*
1   *clove garlic, minced*
¼   *cup white wine*
2   *tablespoons tomato paste diluted with 2 tablespoons water*
1   *bay leaf*
     Salt and pepper

To clean squid, cut off heads and remove bones and food tubes. Wash out ink and remove outer skin, starting at the fins. Wash and slice in 2-inch squares.

Flour pieces lightly and sauté in oil with garlic. Add wine and cover for 3 minutes. Add diluted tomato paste, bay leaf, salt and pepper to taste. Cover and simmer 1 hour, adding broth or wine as necessary, and stirring from time to time to prevent sticking.

CRAB CIOPPINO

2   *live crabs*
4   *tablespoons butter*
4   *tablespoons olive oil*
1   *onion, finely chopped*
2   *salmon bellies, cut in serving pieces*
2   *pounds fresh fish, your choice, cut in serving pieces*
1½   *pounds fresh clams in shells, washed well*
¾   *cup tomato sauce*
½   *cup white wine*
2   *large cloves garlic, minced*
½   *teaspoon rosemary leaves*
2   *tablespoons parsley, finely chopped*
     Salt and pepper

Split crabs with cleaver, wash and clean under running water. Remove claws, divide at joints and crack with mallet. Cut and crack crab into serving pieces with the shells.

Place in baking dish with butter, oil and onion. Arrange salmon, fish and clams around crab. Pour tomato sauce and wine over all. Sprinkle with garlic, rosemary, parsley, salt and pepper to taste. Bake uncovered in 350° oven 45 minutes, basting with pan juices.

Serve in large soup plates with plenty of crusty Italian bread to sop up the juices.

CIOPPINO #2

READY TRAY   Serves 6

1	onion, chopped
1	green bell pepper, chopped
1	carrot, chopped
2	stalks celery, chopped
1/4	cup olive oil
2	cups dry white or red wine
2	cups whole-pack tomatoes, chopped
1	cup water
1/4	cup parsley, finely chopped
1	teaspoon oregano leaves
2	cloves garlic, mashed
	Salt and pepper
3	pounds assorted fish, including salmon bellies, cut in 2-inch pieces
1	crab, with shell cracked and cleaned
12	shrimp with shells
12	clams in shells
12	oysters in shells

Sauté onion, green pepper, carrot and celery in oil until wilted. Add wine, tomatoes, water, parsley, oregano, garlic, salt and pepper to taste. Cover and simmer 40 minutes.

Wash and clean fish, crab and shrimp. Place in a large kettle, pour hot sauce over, cover and simmer until tender, 35 minutes.

Add washed clams and oysters to hot sauce and as soon as they open in their shells, the dish is ready. Serve in soup plates, with crusty pieces of Italian bread to dunk in the sauce.

130

FISH AND HERBS

READY TRAY   Serves 4 to 6

1   whole fish your choice, approximately 4 pounds,
    scaled and cleaned
1   large onion, chopped
    Salt and pepper
2   stalks celery, chopped
1   cup sliced fresh mushrooms
1   tablespoon chopped parsley
1   teaspoon fresh thyme, chopped
1   teaspoon fresh rosemary leaves, chopped
4   tablespoons olive oil
½   cup dry white wine
    Grated Parmesan cheese

> Season fish with salt and pepper to taste.
> Combine all ingredients except fish, cheese and wine.
> Spread half of chopped vegetables and herbs on bottom
> of baking dish. Place fish on top. Sprinkle lightly with
> cheese and cover with remainder of mixture.
> Bake uncovered in 375° oven 40 minutes or longer,
> until tender and flaky. Baste with pan juices, adding
> wine to baking dish about 10 to 15 minutes before done,
> since more liquid may be needed.

LOBSTER FRA DIAVOLO

READY TRAY   Serves 2

1   lobster, cleaned and split in half lengthwise
1   clove garlic, minced
1   tablespoon parsley, minced
4   tablespoons butter
1   tablespoon olive oil
½   cup tomato sauce
2   red chili peppers, minced
1   teaspoon oregano
    Salt and pepper
1   tablespoon grated Parmesan cheese
2   tablespoons white wine

> Place split lobsters and claws in hot oven (400°) for
> 10 minutes. Remove meat, break into bite-size pieces and

131

set aside. Be sure not to break the large outer shells.

Brown garlic and parsley in butter and oil. Add tomato sauce, chili peppers, oregano, salt and pepper to taste. Simmer 5 minutes. Remove from heat, add lobster meat, cheese and wine. Blend well and fill lobster shells with the mixture. Bake uncovered in 300° oven for 25 minutes.

SCAMPI IN WINE

READY TRAY Serves 2 to 4

1   *pound large fresh shrimp, shelled and cleaned, with tails left on*
¼   *pound butter*
1   *large clove garlic, finely chopped*
2   *teaspoons parsley, finely chopped*
    Juice of 1 lemon
⅓   *cup white wine*
    Salt and pepper

Scampi are the very large shrimp found in the Mediterranean waters.

Melt butter, add garlic and parsley, and brown lightly. Blend in lemon juice, wine, salt and pepper to taste. Add shrimp and sauté quickly, stirring until tender 5 minutes.

Serve sauce over shrimps.

BROILED SHRIMPS

READY TRAY Serves 4 to 6

2   *pounds shrimp, washed thoroughly and unshelled*
2   *cloves garlic*
10 *whole peppercorns*
    Salt
4   *tablespoons parsley, finely chopped*
1   *cup olive oil*

Mash garlic with peppercorns thoroughly. Blend in salt to taste, parsley and oil.

Dip unshelled shrimp in sauce and place in broiling pan. Pour remaining sauce over shrimps and broil 8 to 10 minutes until tender. Serve with sauce.

(The shrimp may be shelled, cleaned and deveined, with the tails left on.)

132

FILLET OF SOLE AND TOMATOES

Serves 4 to 6

8   fillets of sole
    Salt and pepper
1   onion, chopped
1   scallion, chopped
1   clove garlic, chopped
4   tablespoons olive oil
2   tablespoons flour
1   cup dry white wine
½   cup light cream
3   tomatoes, peeled, seeded and chopped
1   tablespoon parsley, finely chopped
1   teaspoon fresh basil, finely chopped
    Salt and pepper
½   cup breadcrumbs
¼   cup grated Parmesan cheese

Place fish in buttered baking dish. Salt and pepper to taste.

Brown onion, scallion and garlic in oil lightly. Stir in flour, gradually pour in wine, bring to boil. Reduce heat and slowly add cream. Simmer 5 minutes. Then add tomatoes, parsley, basil, salt and pepper to taste, blend well and pour sauce over fish. Sprinkle with breadcrumbs and cheese. Bake uncovered in 375° oven 25 minutes until fish is tender and top is browned lightly.

Salse

Salse simply means sauces. The Italian form of the word is used in order to distinguish the sauce recipes in this chapter from the tomato and meat sauces used in the preparation of pasta dishes (Sauces for Pasta).

The recipes call for combinations of herbs, roots, leaves, fruits, seeds, vinegar, wine, oil and salt blended together. They can be prepared quickly; many require no cooking, and others just a short period of cooking. Some are very good to use when basting, roasting or barbecuing meats. Others are served with broiled or boiled meat or fish to give it flavor and zest.

ANCHOVY AND CAPER SALSA

READY TRAY

2   *tablespoons pickled capers*
4   *anchovy fillets*
2   *tablespoons olive oil*

       Mince capers and anchovies together thoroughly. Heat in oil, but do not allow to boil.
       This is very good on boiled tongue.

CHICKEN SALSA

READY TRAY

½   *cup Italian truffles, chopped*
2   *tablespoons onion, minced*
2   *tablespoons veal, minced*
4   *tablespoons butter*
1   *tablespoon brandy*
2   *tablespoons flour*
1   *cup heavy fresh cream*
1   *cup milk*
    Pinch fresh thyme leaves
⅛   *teaspoon fresh grated nutmeg*
    Salt and pepper

Sauté truffles, onion and veal in butter until onion is golden brown. Add brandy and flour, and stir thoroughly. Reduce heat to low, and gradually add cream combined with milk, stirring until smooth. Blend in thyme, nutmeg, salt and pepper to taste.

Excellent served over any type of cooked chicken.

MEAT AND CHOPS SALSA

READY TRAY

1	teaspoon flour
1	teaspoon vinegar
3	green onions, minced
¼	cup butter
¼	cup pickled capers
¼	cup pitted ripe olives, finely chopped
3	anchovy fillets, finely chopped

Blend flour and vinegar together to form a paste.

Brown onions in butter over medium heat. Add capers, olives, the vinegar and flour paste, and simmer gently for 3 minutes. Remove from heat. Add anchovies and mash with a fork into a thick paste.

If it becomes too thick, this sauce can be thinned by adding a little boiling water or broth.

BOILED FISH SALSA

READY TRAY

2	tablespoons butter
1	teaspoon flour
½	cup fish broth
1	egg yolk, beaten lightly
1	tablespoon fresh lemon juice
	Salt and pepper

Melt butter over low heat. Stir in flour until light golden brown. Add fish broth slowly and stir 4 minutes. Remove from heat. Blend in beaten egg yolk and lemon juice slowly until well mixed. Add salt and pepper to taste.

BAKED FISH SALSA

READY TRAY

4   *hard-cooked egg yolks, minced*
8   *anchovy fillets, minced*
2   *tablespoons olive oil*
1   *tablespoon lemon juice*

Mash egg yolks and anchovies together. Add oil, a little at a time, until the mixture is creamy. Add lemon juice and blend well.

CAPERS AND BUTTER SALSA

READY TRAY

¼   *pound sweet butter*
⅓   *cup capers*
1   *tablespoon lemon juice*
    Salt

Melt butter. Add capers, lemon juice and salt to taste, but use salt sparingly because capers are a little salty. Serve with vegetables or fish.

PIQUANT SALSA

READY TRAY

4   *anchovy fillets*
2   *tablespoons pickled capers*
2   *spring green onions, white part only*
2   *cloves garlic*
1   *teaspoon basil*
2   *tablespoons olive oil*
1   *tablespoon parsley, finely chopped*
    Juice of ½ lemon
    Salt and pepper

Mince together the anchovies, capers, onions, garlic and basil to make a thick paste. Use a mortar and pestle to do this or an electric blender.

Add oil, parsley, lemon juice, salt (sparingly) and pepper to taste.

Delicious with hot or cold meats or fish.

PROSCIUTTO SALSA

READY TRAY

1   *small onion*
1   *tablespoon pickled capers*
1   *slice prosciutto, ¼ inch thick*
2   *tablespoons olive oil*
1   *teaspoon basil*
1   *tablespoon parsley, finely chopped*
2   *tablespoons stock or broth*
    Juice of ½ lemon
4   *anchovy fillets, finely chopped*
    Black pepper

Mince together onion, capers and prosciutto, and brown in oil over low heat. Add basil, parsley and stock. Remove from heat, add lemon juice and anchovies, and blend thoroughly. Season to taste with pepper.

Serve with steaks, boiled meats or fish.

HUNTER-STYLE SALSA

READY TRAY

½   *cup white wine*
½   *cup meat stock or broth*
    Juice of 1 lemon
2   *tablespoons olive oil*
1   *sprig fresh rosemary*
½   *cup fine breadcrumbs*
2   *green onions, minced*
1   *tablespoon parsley, finely chopped*
    Pinch of nutmeg
    Salt and pepper to taste

Place all ingredients in a saucepan over medium heat. Bring to slow boil, cook 5 minutes. Remove from heat.

Good with all game.

BROILED MEAT SALSA

2   tablespoons chopped parsley
1   clove garlic, minced
2   tablespoons olive oil
1   tablespoon tomato paste
1   tablespoon broth or water
6   peperoncini, stems and seeds removed, chopped
4   anchovy fillets, chopped
    Pepper

Sauté parsley and garlic in oil quickly. Add tomato paste diluted with broth and boil 2 minutes.

Add peperoncini, anchovies and pepper to taste. Heat thoroughly, but do not boil.

Good for basting broiled meats or fish.

MINT SALSA

1   handful tender fresh mint leaves
⅔   cup vinegar
⅓   cup water
2   tablespoons sugar
½   teaspoon salt

Wash mint thoroughly and drain. Chop coarsely and put in a jar.

Combine vinegar and water with sugar and salt; stir until dissolved. Pour over chopped mint and let sit 3 hours before serving over roast lamb.

STEAK SALSA

1   clove garlic, minced
1   tablespoon parsley, minced
2   tablespoons butter
1   teaspoon lemon juice
    Salt and pepper to taste

Place all ingredients in small frying pan and mash them thoroughly with a fork. Simmer until butter is melted.

Serve over steaks.

SWEET AND SOUR SALSA

READY TRAY

2   tablespoons pine nuts
2   tablespoons raisins
2   tablespoons grated sweet chocolate
2   tablespoons candied orange and grapefruit rinds, minced
½   cup sugar
⅓   cup vinegar

Mix all ingredients and boil slowly 10 minutes.

Serve over boiled meat. Meat may be placed in salsa and heated in it, if desired.

FRESH TOMATO SALSA

READY TRAY

6   ripe tomatoes, peeled and finely chopped
2   tablespoons fresh basil, finely chopped
3   cloves garlic, gently crushed
    Salt and pepper
½   cup olive oil

Combine tomatoes, basil, garlic, salt and pepper to taste. Pour oil over top, cover and chill several hours. Discard garlic before serving over cold meats or shellfish.

This salsa may also be heated thoroughly and served with a favorite pasta.

RADISH SALSA

READY TRAY

4   tablespoons grated radishes
1   pint sour cream
    Salt and pepper

Simmer sour cream 2 minutes. Add grated radishes, salt and pepper to taste. Remove from heat, stirring with a wooden spoon 1 minute.

Serve hot with boiled fish.

TRUFFLE SALSA

READY TRAY

2	truffles, sliced very thin
2	green onions, minced
1	clove garlic, minced
1	teaspoon parsley, minced
2	tablespoons butter
¼	cup white wine
1	teaspoon flour
	Pinch allspice
	Salt and pepper
2	tablespoons broth

Sauté onions, garlic and parsley in butter until golden brown. Add wine blended with flour, salt and pepper to taste and allspice. Stir gently as it thickens. Add truffles, heat thoroughly but do not boil.

If truffles are not available, fresh button mushrooms sliced thinly may be substituted.

This is an excellent salsa for steaks, veal cutlets and roasts.

TUNA SALSA

READY TRAY

1	4-ounce can of tuna
4	anchovy fillets
2	tablespoons olive oil
4	tablespoons pickled capers
	Juice of 1 lemon

Mince tuna and anchovies together thoroughly. Add oil and blend into a thick paste. Add capers and lemon juice and mix well before serving.

Delicious with hot or cold meats.

140

VINAIGRETTE SALSA

2   *tablespoons minced onion*
1   *tablespoon olive oil*
1   *tablespoon minced capers*
3   *tablespoons minced parsley*
1   *small dill pickle, minced*
2   *tablespoons white wine vinegar*
1   *tablespoon sugar*
   Salt and pepper to taste

> Brown onion in oil. Add remaining ingredients and simmer 5 minutes.
> Use hot or cold over roast lamb.

MUSHROOM SALSA

½   *pound fresh mushrooms, sliced thin*
3   *tablespoons butter*
1   *tablespoon fresh tarragon leaves, finely chopped*
1   *clove garlic, minced*
½   *cup red wine*
   Salt and pepper

> Sauté mushrooms lightly in butter until wilted. Add tarragon, garlic, wine, salt and pepper to taste. Heat thoroughly.
> Excellent with any kind of chops or a London broil.

Vegetables

A beautiful picture is the fresh vegetable counter in your supermarket, and if there is a fruit and vegetable store in your neighborhood, then you are fortunate indeed. Those mounds of vegetables and fruits, of every color and size, are a work of art and a challenge to the cook!

In this day of frozen vegetables, if you see a vegetable in its fresh state that you haven't eaten lately, try it! Frozen is good, but fresh is better. And the work of preparing and cleaning the vegetable is forgotten when you taste the fresh asparagus or spinach or broccoli.

The Italians eat vegetables in abundance, and a classic dressing for the boiled vegetable is oil, lemon, salt and pepper added at the table by the individual. The secret is not to overcook. A vegetable is done when it is, like pasta, al dente—cooked but firm to the bite.

Many of the recipes in this chapter are in fact casseroles, using rice or a little meat or eggs, to turn them into dishes substantial enough to serve as a luncheon course.

STUFFED ARTICHOKES

READY TRAY   Serves 4 to 6

12   artichokes
1   lemon, cut in half
¼   cup vinegar
1   cup breadcrumbs
4   anchovy fillets, finely chopped
¼   cup grated Parmesan cheese
4   tablespoons parsley, minced
2   cloves garlic, minced
     Salt and pepper
1   tablespoon olive oil

The best artichokes to stuff are small ones, about 2 inches in diameter. Discard the outer leaves. Trim tops flat across and cut off stems.

Add vinegar to one quart water. Rub each artichoke with cut lemon and drop in vinegar-water to keep them from darkening.

142

Combine breadcrumbs, anchovies, cheese, parsley, garlic, salt and pepper to taste.

Drain artichokes and loosen leaves by gently pressing out. Place a little dressing in between the leaves.

Place artichokes in shallow baking dish, close together, in upright position. Sprinkle remainder of dressing over them. Pour ¼ teaspoon oil over each artichoke. Add 1 cup hot water to bottom of baking dish and bake uncovered in 350° oven, approximately 40 minutes, until tender.

ASPARAGUS AND RICE IN CASSEROLE

READY TRAY   Serves 4 to 6

2   *pounds fresh asparagus*
½   *cup raw rice*
1   *onion, chopped*
2   *tablespoons olive oil*
1   *tablespoon lemon juice*
     Salt and pepper to taste
2   *eggs, beaten*
1   *teaspoon tarragon leaves*
2   *tablespoons grated Parmesan cheese*

Cut asparagus in 2-inch lengths and steam in salted water, just enough to cover. Cook until tender but not soft.

Cook rice and drain thoroughly. Brown onion in oil. Then combine all ingredients carefully and place into a buttered casserole. Bake uncovered in 350° oven 25 minutes.

FRIED ARTICHOKES

READY TRAY   Serves 4

6   *artichokes*
     Salt and pepper
     Flour
1   *egg, lightly beaten*
1   *cup breadcrumbs*
     Olive oil

143

Remove outer leaves. Trim tops flat and split or quarter the whole artichokes, according to their size, in pieces about 1 inch across. Remove silky centers.

Salt and pepper to taste. Flour lightly, dip in beaten egg, roll in breadcrumbs and fry in hot oil until golden brown.

Cauliflower, celery and cardone can be prepared in this same manner.

BOILED ARTICHOKES

READY TRAY   Serves 4

4   artichokes
    Salt
1   teaspoon olive oil
½   fresh lemon
        or
1   tablespoon vinegar
    Mayonnaise

Cover artichokes with salted cold water and soak one hour. Remove tough outer leaves and stems.

Bring 1 quart of water to boil, adding 1 teaspoon salt, oil, lemon or vinegar to water. Add artichokes and cook until tender, approximately 40 minutes. Drain and serve with side dish of mayonnaise for dipping leaves.

This makes a very good antipasto course.

ASPARAGUS PARMESAN

READY TRAY   Serves 4

1   bunch asparagus
4   tablespoons grated Parmesan cheese
4   tablespoons butter
    Salt and pepper

Clean asparagus and cook in salted water until just tender, not too soft. Drain and place in a shallow baking dish.

Season with pepper and sprinkle with cheese. Dot top with butter and bake uncovered in 350° oven, 10 minutes.

GARBANZO BEANS

1   *pound dried garbanzo beans, soaked overnight*
2   *cloves garlic, finely chopped*
1   *onion, finely chopped*
⅓   *cup olive oil*
2   *cups whole-pack tomatoes, chopped*
1   *can pimientos, cut in strips*
    Salt and pepper

> Drain beans and cover with water. Add garlic, onion and oil. Cover and cook gently 1 hour. Add tomatoes and simmer until beans are tender and tomatoes have cooked down. During last 15 minutes of cooking, add pimientos and season to taste with salt and pepper.

STRING BEANS

1   *pound tender string beans, cut in 3-inch lengths*
1   *onion, finely chopped*
1   *clove garlic, minced*
¼   *cup olive oil*
2   *ripe tomatoes, peeled and finely chopped*
    Salt and pepper

> Brown onion and garlic in oil. Add beans, tomatoes, salt and pepper to taste and enough hot water to cover. Cover saucepan and cook slowly until almost tender. Remove cover and simmer until liquid is absorbed.

BABY LIMA BEANS

1   *pound fresh lima beans, shelled*
1   *onion, finely chopped*
¼   *cup olive oil*
1   *ripe tomato, peeled and chopped*
6   *fresh or dried sage leaves*
    Salt and pepper

Brown onion in oil. Add tomato, lima beans, sage leaves, salt and pepper to taste. Add enough hot water to cover. Cover and cook over medium heat until tender.

ITALIAN BEANS PARMESAN

READY TRAY   Serves 4

1 pound Italian green beans
6 tablespoons butter
2 tablespoons flour
¾ cup milk
   Salt
   Pinch fresh grated nutmeg
2 eggs, beaten
2 tablespoons grated Parmesan cheese
1 cup breadcrumbs

Cook beans in water to cover until tender. Drain and cut in 2-inch lengths. Add 2 tablespoons butter and set aside.

Blend remaining butter with flour over low heat. Gradually add milk and cook until sauce is smooth and thick. Salt to taste and add nutmeg. Add eggs and cheese and stir until well blended. Combine sauce with beans.

Butter a deep casserole and use part of breadcrumbs to coat sides of the casserole. Pour beans with sauce into casserole, sprinkle with remaining breadcrumbs and bake in 400° oven, 30 minutes.

ITALIAN GREEN BEANS

READY TRAY   Serves 6

2 packages frozen Italian green beans
3 tablespoons slivered blanched almonds
3 tablespoons butter
   Salt and freshly ground black pepper

Cook beans per directions, until tender. Drain and place beans in heated serving dish. Season to taste with salt and pepper.

Brown almonds lightly in butter over low heat. Pour over beans and serve immediately.

STRING BEANS AND ARTICHOKE HEARTS

READY TRAY   Serves 4

1 *pound string beans*
1 *tablespoon butter*
8 *artichoke hearts, canned and drained*
   Salt and pepper

> Cook string beans in salted water to cover until tender, leaving the beans whole. Drain, add butter and shake well. Add artichoke hearts and heat thoroughly over low heat. Salt and pepper to taste before serving.

STRING BEANS WITH PROSCIUTTO

READY TRAY   Serves 4

1 *pound string beans, cut in 2-inch lengths*
   Salt
4 *tablespoons butter*
¼ *pound thinly sliced prosciutto, cut in ½-inch strips*

> Cook string beans in salted water until tender. Drain. Melt butter, add beans and stir gently. Add prosciutto and heat thoroughly.

CARDONI WITH SAUSAGE

READY TRAY   Serves 4

2 *stalks cardoni, cooked, drained and cut in 4-inch lengths*
¼ *cup butter, melted*
2 *links fresh sausage, thinly sliced*
¼ *cup grated Parmesan cheese*
⅛ *teaspoon allspice*
   Salt and pepper

> Place cooked cardoni in shallow baking dish with the butter. Arrange sausage slices on top, sprinkle with cheese, allspice, salt and pepper to taste.
> Bake uncovered in 325° oven 30 minutes, until sausage is cooked.

BROCCOLI AND GARLIC

READY TRAY   Serves 4

    1   bunch broccoli
    ¼   cup olive oil
    2   cloves garlic, minced

       Cover broccoli with salted water and cook until tender.
Drain; break sprouts and stems into walnut-size pieces
and set aside.
       Brown garlic in oil quickly. Add broccoli, and stir
gently until oil is well absorbed.
       Swiss chard prepared in this manner is excellent.

CABBAGE AND RICE

READY TRAY   Serves 4 to 6

    1   head cabbage, chopped, steamed and drained
    1   cup cooked rice
    1   teaspoon chopped parsley
    1   teaspoon fennel seeds
    ½   cup chopped pine nuts
    2   tablespoons white wine
        Salt and pepper

       Place half the cabbage in a buttered casserole. Cover
with rice, parsley, fennel seeds, pine nuts. Sprinkle with
wine, add salt and pepper to taste, and spread remainder
of chopped cabbage over top. Bake uncovered in 325°
oven, 30 minutes, until heated thoroughly.

SAUTÉED CUCUMBERS

READY TRAY   Serves 4

    4   cucumbers
    3   tablespoons butter or olive oil
        Salt
    ½   teaspoon sugar
    1   tablespoon parsley, finely chopped

Peel cucumbers, cut in half lengthwise, remove seeds and slice halves in 1-inch lengths. Parboil in salted water to cover, 10 minutes.

Drain thoroughly and sauté cucumbers in butter or oil, first sprinkling them with sugar, until golden brown. Sprinkle with parsley before serving.

CAULIFLOWER IN CASSEROLE

READY TRAY   Serves 4

1   large head cauliflower, broken into flowerets
¼   pound prosciutto, diced
2   hard-cooked eggs, diced
¼   cup grated Parmesan cheese
¼   cup breadcrumbs
       Salt and pepper to taste
1   tablespoon minced parsley
1   clove garlic, minced
3   tablespoons butter

Cook cauliflower in salted water until tender. Drain and place in buttered casserole.

Combine all ingredients, except butter, and sprinkle over cauliflower. Dot with butter. Bake uncovered in 350° oven, 15 to 20 minutes.

CELERY IN CASSEROLE

READY TRAY   Serves 4 to 6

2   bunches celery
       Flour
2   eggs, lightly beaten
½   cup olive oil
4   tablespoons butter
1   cup breadcrumbs
¼   cup grated Parmesan or Romano cheese
       Salt and pepper
       Butter
⅓   cup broth

Cut off tops of celery, removing leaves, and trim. Cut celery stalks in 4-inch lengths. Parboil in salted water

149

5 minutes. Place in cold water to cover, to cool.

Drain, dip in flour, then into beaten eggs. Fry in oil until golden brown. Arrange in layers in a deep casserole, sprinkling each layer with breadcrumbs, grated cheese, a little pepper and dots of butter. Pour broth over top. Bake uncovered in 325° oven, 30 minutes.

FRIED EGGPLANT

READY TRAY   Serves 4

2   *eggplants, sliced ½ inch thick, with skin left on*
    Salt and pepper
1   *egg, lightly beaten*
    Flour
¼   *cup olive oil*
1   *cup tomato sauce, heated thoroughly*
4   *tablespoons grated Parmesan cheese*

Salt and pepper eggplant slices to taste. Dip in egg, then in flour and brown in hot oil. Arrange slices on heated serving platter, pour tomato sauce over them, sprinkle with cheese and serve.

EGGPLANT AND LAMB

READY TRAY   Serves 4 to 6

2   *eggplants, peeled, sliced 1 inch thick in rounds*
½   *cup olive oil*
2   *onions, finely chopped*
2   *tablespoons butter*
2   *cloves garlic, finely chopped*
1   *pound ground lamb*
1   *large can whole-pack tomatoes, chopped*
1   *cup tomato sauce*
1   *teaspoon basil leaves*
    Salt and pepper
    Grated Romano cheese

Sauté eggplant slices in oil until evenly browned on both sides. Sauté onions in butter with garlic and meat until well browned. Add tomatoes, sauce, basil, salt and pepper to taste, and simmer 25 minutes.

Arrange in casserole in alternate layers the eggplant slices and meat. Sprinkle each layer with cheese. Bake uncovered in 350° oven, 35 minutes.

EGGPLANT WITH PROSCIUTTO

READY TRAY   Serves 4 to 6

2   *eggplants, sliced ½ inch thick, skin left on*
    Salt and pepper
    Flour
½   *cup olive oil*
2   *cups marinara tomato sauce*
6   *thin slices prosciutto*
6   *thin slices mozzarella cheese*

Salt and pepper eggplant slices to taste. Dust lightly with flour, and brown in oil quickly.

Pour ⅓ cup tomato sauce over bottom of large baking dish. Arrange alternate layers of browned eggplant, tomato sauce, prosciutto and cheese. Bake uncovered in 350° oven, 40 minutes.

STUFFED EGGPLANT

READY TRAY   Serves 4

1   *eggplant, cut in half lengthwise*
¼   *cup butter*
3   *green onions, chopped*
1   *clove garlic, minced*
1   *thin slice prosciutto, diced*
1   *tablespoon parsley, minced*
¼   *cup grated Parmesan cheese*
2   *pinches dried basil*
    Salt and pepper
1   *egg, beaten*
1   *tablespoon breadcrumbs*
4   *slices tomato*

151

Parboil eggplant in salted water 10 minutes. Spoon out pulp, leaving ¼-inch-thick shell, and chop pulp.

Brown the onions and garlic lightly in butter. Add chopped eggplant, prosciutto, parsley, cheese, basil, salt and pepper to taste. Heat thoroughly. Blend in beaten egg.

Fill eggplant shells, sprinkle with breadcrumbs and cheese. Place 2 slices of tomato on each half shell and bake in 350° oven, 40 minutes.

FRESH FAVA BEANS

The Fava beans were the only beans the Old World knew before the discovery of the Americas. It is commonly known as the broad bean, the Windsor bean or the horse bean.

The beans are tastiest when fresh. The dried beans are boiled until tender, the skins are removed and they are mashed with oil or butter, until they have a consistency like that of mashed potatoes.

READY TRAY

1   *pound tender fava beans, shelled*
1   *onion, finely chopped*
4   *tablespoons butter*
1   *tablespoon oil*
    Salt and pepper

Brown onions in butter and oil. Add the fava beans, with salt and pepper to taste, and stir until butter is absorbed. Add small amount hot water, cover and cook over low heat until tender.

Quartered artichokes can be added and cooked together with the fava beans.

FENNEL

Fennel is a very aromatic plant which is eaten raw, like celery, in central Italy. Its seeds have the odor of anise, and should be used sparingly as a seasoning, since they impart a very strong flavor.

152

3   *heads fennel*
5   *tablespoons butter*
2   *tablespoons broth*
1   *teaspoon flour*
    Salt
3   *tablespoons grated Parmesan cheese*

Trim fennel and discard outer leaves. Slice heads lengthwise in ½-inch-wide strips. Parboil 5 minutes, drain and dry. Sauté strips in 4 tablespoons butter, add broth, with salt to taste, then cover and simmer until tender.

Blend 1 tablespoon butter with flour and add to fennel, stirring until smooth. Sprinkle with cheese before serving.

CHICK-PEAS (CECI) MARINARA

¼   *cup butter*
4   *anchovy fillets, finely chopped*
2   *cups cooked chick-peas with a little liquid*
    Salt and pepper
1   *teaspoon parsley, finely chopped*

Melt butter, add anchovies, chick-peas, salt and pepper to taste and parsley. Use salt sparingly.

Heat thoroughly before serving.

FRIED PEPPERS

1   *pound fresh peppers, your choice*
¼   *cup olive oil*
2   *cloves garlic, finely chopped*
    Salt and pepper
    Lemon wedges

Place peppers in a hot oven until skins wrinkle. Remove skins, stems and seeds. Cut lengthwise in 4-inch strips.

Place pepper slices in hot oil with garlic, salt and pepper to taste, and fry until tender, about 15 minutes. Serve with lemon wedges.

BRUSSELS SPROUTS WITH MUSHROOMS

READY TRAY   Serves 4 to 6

4   *cups Brussels sprouts*
4   *tablespoons olive oil*
½   *pound fresh mushrooms, sliced*
     Salt and pepper
     Juice of 1 lemon
1   *tablespoon parsley, finely chopped*

Steam sprouts in salted water to cover until tender; drain thoroughly.

Sauté mushrooms in oil until wilted. Add sprouts, salt and pepper to taste and lemon juice. Toss lightly and sprinkle with parsley before serving.

LEAF VEGETABLES WITH GARLIC

READY TRAY   Serves 4

1   *pound leaf vegetable, your choice—spinach, escarole, endive*
3   *tablespoons olive oil*
2   *cloves garlic, minced*
     Lemon wedges
            or
     Vinegar

Clean greens thoroughly. Boil escarole or endive in salted water to cover and drain thoroughly. Spinach requires only a small amount of water and kettle should be covered, since the spinach is actually steamed, not boiled, in a matter of minutes.

Brown garlic in oil lightly. Add drained greens and stir to coat with a delicate film of oil.

Serve with lemon wedges or vinegar.

154

MAMA ROSSI'S GARDEN TREAT

Serves 6 to 8

2   onions, thinly sliced in rounds
4   stalks celery, cut in 2-inch lengths
2   potatoes, thinly sliced
3   carrots, thinly sliced
1   No. 2 can whole-pack tomatoes, chopped, liquid reserved
1   bunch Swiss chard, cut in 2-inch lengths
1   pound zucchini, thinly sliced
    Salt and pepper
1   cup grated Parmesan cheese
½   cup finely chopped parsley
¼   pound butter

Arrange vegetables in large buttered casserole in layers, with salt and pepper to taste. Sprinkle cheese and parsley evenly over each layer. Dot top with butter, pour reserve tomato juice over layers, cover and bake in 350° oven 1 hour.

When in season, leaf vegetables, eggplant, hot or sweet peppers may be added to this dish.

STUFFED ONIONS

Serves 4 to 6

6   large onions, peeled
2   tablespoons butter, melted
3   cups soft breadcrumbs
    Olive oil
½   pound ground beef
1   egg yolk
2   teaspoons parsley, finely chopped
    Salt and pepper
¼   teaspoon marjoram

Cut off root end and ½-inch slice from tops of onions. Parboil 10 minutes in salted water to cover. Drain and cool. Scoop out centers, leaving 3 layers of onion. Chop up centers.
Combine melted butter with 1 cup breadcrumbs and set aside. Blend chopped onions with 2 tablespoons olive

oil and meat, and brown thoroughly, breaking meat
into small pieces as it browns. Add remainder of breadcrumbs, egg yolk, 1 teaspoon parsley, salt and pepper to
taste and marjoram.

Fill onions with mixture and place in casserole.
Sprinkle tops with buttered crumbs, a little oil and
remainder of parsley. Bake uncovered in 350° oven,
40 minutes.

STUFFED SQUASH

Serves 4

3   crookneck squash
     Salt and pepper
1   onion, finely chopped
1   clove garlic, finely chopped
2   tablespoons butter or oil
1   cup breadcrumbs
1   teaspoon lemon juice
     Pinch ground hot chili peppers
¼   cup grated Parmesan cheese

Steam squash until tender. Cool, cut in half lengthwise, scoop out centers, leaving shells intact. Salt and
pepper to taste and chop centers.

Sauté onions and garlic in butter or oil until golden
brown. Add breadcrumbs, lemon juice, chili pepper and
cheese and chopped squash pulp. Fill shells with mixture
and bake uncovered in 425° oven, 20 minutes.

STUFFED MUSHROOMS

Serves 4

1   pound large fresh mushrooms, wiped with damp cloth
1   slice prosciutto, minced
2   tablespoons grated Parmesan cheese
2   tablespoons breadcrumbs
1   tablespoon parsley, minced
     Salt and pepper
1   egg
¼   cup olive oil

Remove stems from mushroom caps and chop up fine. Combine prosciutto, cheese, breadcrumbs, mushroom stems, parsley, salt and pepper to taste and egg.

Spread dressing evenly inside the mushroom caps. Place in single layer in a baking dish, and pour oil over the top. Add ¼ cup hot water to baking dish. Bake uncovered in 300° oven, 25 to 30 minutes.

MUSHROOMS AND HERBS

READY TRAY   Serves 4 to 6

1   pound fresh mushrooms, sliced
6   green onions, sliced
¼   cup olive oil
¼   cup broth
½   teaspoon oregano
½   teaspoon marjoram
    Salt and pepper
1   tablespoon parsley, finely chopped

Sauté mushrooms and onions in oil until wilted. Add broth, oregano, marjoram, salt and pepper to taste and parsley.

Turn into casserole, bake in 350° oven, covered, for 20 to 25 minutes.

ZUCCHINI AND TOMATOES IN CASSEROLE

READY TRAY   Serves 4 to 6

4   zucchini, unpeeled, sliced ½ inch thick in rounds
2   green bell peppers, seeded, cut in 1-inch squares
4   tomatoes, sliced ½ inch thick
2   sweet onions, sliced ¼ inch thick
½   teaspoon oregano
½   teaspoon basil
    Salt and pepper
⅓   cup olive oil

Arrange vegetables in alternate layers in deep casserole. Sprinkle with herbs, salt and pepper to taste. Pour oil over top and bake uncovered in 325° oven, 30 to 40 minutes, until tender.

157

ZUCCHINI IN TOMATO SAUCE

4   zucchini, sliced ¾ inch thick, crosswise
1   onion, finely chopped
1   slice prosciutto, finely chopped
2   tablespoons olive oil
1   tablespoon minced parsley
¼   cup tomato sauce
     Salt and pepper
¼   cup grated Parmesan cheese

> Brown onions and prosciutto in oil. Add zucchini, parsley, tomato sauce, salt and pepper to taste. Cover and simmer 15 minutes, stirring occasionally.
>
> Uncover and continue simmering until liquid is almost evaporated. Sprinkle with cheese before serving.

FRIED ZUCCHINI

4   zucchini, sliced ⅜ inch thick
     Flour
4   tablespoons butter
2   tablespoons olive oil
2   cloves garlic, finely chopped
     Salt and pepper
     Oregano

> Flour zucchini lightly and fry slices in butter and oil, with garlic, until tender. Season to taste with salt and pepper. Sprinkle with oregano before serving.

FRESH PEAS, PEASANT STYLE

1   onion, minced
1   slice prosciutto, ½ inch thick, cut in ½-inch cubes
4   tablespoons butter
1   pound fresh or frozen peas
     Salt and pepper

Braise onions and prosciutto in butter. Add peas, salt and pepper to taste and enough hot water to barely cover peas. Cook covered over medium heat, 10 minutes. Remove cover, reduce heat and stir until most of the liquid is absorbed.

ZUCCHINI AND EGGS

READY TRAY

4 *zucchini*
Flour
4 *tablespoons butter*
2 *tablespoons olive oil*
Salt and pepper
2 *eggs, lightly beaten*
1 *tablespoon cold water*
Grated Parmesan cheese

Cut zucchini in half, then split each half lengthwise in 4 pieces. Flour lightly and brown evenly in butter and oil. Salt and pepper to taste.

Pour eggs beaten with water evenly over top and cook until set. Serve with cheese sprinkled over the top.

Eggs

What can be said about the egg that hasn't already been said? It is one item the cook is usually sure to have on hand, and alone or with other ingredients, depending on the creative mood of the cook, a dish that will be freshly cooked and delicious can quickly be prepared.

EGGS AND CHICKEN LIVERS

READY TRAY   Serves 4

1   *pound chicken livers, cut in half*
6   *tablespoons butter*
    Salt and pepper
1   *cup broth*
2   *egg yolks*
½   *teaspoon flour*
1   *tablespoon lemon juice*
    Trimmed toast

Sauté chicken livers in butter lightly. Salt and pepper to taste. Reduce heat to simmer and add a small amount of broth at a time, simmering until livers are tender.

Blend egg yolks with flour and lemon juice. Stir into chicken livers until thick and smooth. Serve over toast.

EGGS OVER EGGS

READY TRAY   Serves 4 to 6

10   *eggs*
1   *teaspoon capers, finely chopped*
2   *anchovy fillets, finely chopped*
1   *teaspoon minced parsley*
1   *leek, finely chopped*
    Salt and pepper
    Pinch nutmeg.
2   *tablespoons butter*

Separate yolks and whites of 4 eggs. Beat whites until stiff and set aside.

Combine 4 egg yolks with capers, anchovies, parsley, leek, salt and pepper to taste and nutmeg. Carefully fold in whites.

Break the 6 eggs carefully into buttered shallow baking dish. Pour blended egg mixture over the top and bake in 400° oven until set, approximately 10 minutes.

EGGS AND PROSCIUTTO

READY TRAY   Serves 4

2   slices prosciutto, ¼ inch thick, chopped
1   small onion, finely chopped
1   clove garlic, minced
2   tablespoons olive oil
1   cup whole-pack tomatoes, chopped
1   bay leaf
½   teaspoon basil leaves
    Salt and pepper
4–6 eggs
2   tablespoons butter
2   tablespoons grated Romano cheese
3   fresh mint leaves, minced

Sauté prosciutto, onion and garlic in oil until golden brown. Add tomatoes, bay leaf, basil, salt and pepper to taste, and simmer 45 minutes.

Beat eggs with a little salt and pepper until light. Make 4 small omelets and brown lightly on both sides in butter. Cut omelets in 1-inch strips, place in sauce, sprinkle with cheese and mint and cook 5 more minutes.

EGGS IN PURGATORY

READY TRAY   Serves 2

2   cups plain tomato sauce
4   eggs
    Salt and pepper
2   tablespoons grated cheese
1   teaspoon finely chopped parsley

161

Bring tomato sauce to slow boil. Drop in eggs gently, add salt and pepper to taste, sprinkle with cheese and parsley. Cover and simmer over low heat to desired doneness. Serve over toast, if desired, or over crusty Italian bread.

EGGS POACHED WITH TOMATOES

READY TRAY   Serves 3

6   green onions, sliced in ½-inch pieces
4   tablespoons butter
4   tomatoes, peeled and seeded
    Salt and pepper
6   eggs
    Toast

Wilt onions in butter. Add tomatoes, crushing with fork as they cook. Add salt and pepper to taste, and a small amount of hot water to prevent drying out. Simmer 30 minutes.

Break and drop eggs gently on tomatoes. Cover and simmer until eggs are cooked to desired doneness. Serve over toast.

This is an excellent Sunday morning breakfast dish.

EGGS FLORENTINE

READY TRAY   Serves 4 to 6

1   bunch spinach, chopped
2   tablespoons butter
    Salt and pepper
8   eggs
8   slices toast, trimmed
    Anchovy paste
    Grated Parmesan cheese

Cook spinach with butter, with salt and pepper to taste, for 5 minutes. Set aside.

Poach eggs until just set. Spread spinach evenly over toast. Place an egg on each slice of toast, a little anchovy paste and grated cheese over the egg. Bake uncovered in 350° oven, 10 minutes. Serve with additional cheese if desired.

EGGS SUPREME

8   hard-cooked eggs
3   tablespoons butter
2   tablespoons flour
1   cup milk
    Salt and pepper
    Pinch fresh grated nutmeg
1   bunch spinach or Swiss chard leaves, chopped, cooked and drained
    Grated Romano cheese
    Flour
2   eggs, beaten
    Breadcrumbs
    Olive oil

Cut eggs in half, remove and mince yolks. Melt butter, blend in flour until smooth and add milk gradually, stirring until thick. Salt and pepper to taste, and add nutmeg, spinach, egg yolks and cheese. Cool mixture thoroughly until firm. Fill egg whites with mixture, roll them in flour, then in beaten eggs, and again in breadcrumbs. Fry in hot oil until golden brown.

FRITTATA

A *frittata* differs from an omelet in that it is cooked and served flat, whereas an omelet is usually folded in half.

4   eggs
4   tablespoons breadcrumbs
4   tablespoons grated Parmesan cheese
2   tablespoons parsley, minced
2   cloves garlic, minced
    Salt and pepper to taste
2   tablespoons olive oil

Beat eggs thoroughly. Add breadcrumbs, grated cheese, parsley, garlic, salt and pepper.

Heat oil in frying pan. Pour in mixture, flatten and brown lightly on both sides.

The eggs may also be poured into a large buttered

Pyrex pie plate, and baked uncovered in 350° oven until lightly browned on top. Avoid overcooking.

ARTICHOKE FRITTATA

3   artichoke hearts, sliced thin
2   tablespoons butter
    Salt and pepper
2   slices bread, trimmed, soaked and squeezed dry
2   tablespoons grated Parmesan cheese
1   teaspoon chopped fresh marjoram leaves
4   eggs, lightly beaten
1   small clove garlic, minced
    Olive oil

Sauté artichoke hearts in butter lightly. Salt and pepper to taste.

Combine bread, cheese, marjoram, eggs, garlic and artichoke slices. Correct seasoning.

Pour into heated frying pan with 1 tablespoon oil and cook slowly until browned on bottom. Turn carefully and brown top side. Serve in wedge-shaped pieces.

POACHED EGGS DIABLE

2   shallots, minced
4   tablespoons butter
1   tablespoon prepared mustard
½   teaspoon minced parsley
½   teaspoon minced tarragon leaves
½   teaspoon minced chives
     Wine vinegar
1   tablespoon minced onion
3   tablespoons flour
1½   cup milk
1   egg yolk, beaten
2   tablespoons heavy cream
     Salt and pepper
4   eggs, poached
4   slices toast, trimmed and buttered

Sauté shallots in 1 tablespoon butter until golden brown. Add mustard, herbs and a few drops wine vinegar, and set aside. In another saucepan wilt onions in 3 tablespoons butter. Blend in flour and gradually stir in milk until smooth and thick. Stir sauce into sautéed shallots. Add egg yolk beaten with cream, salt and pepper to taste, and cook over hot water until well blended. Do not allow to boil.

Place poached eggs on toast, and cover with sauce.

RICOTTA OMELET

READY TRAY   Serves 4

2   tablespoons flour
2   tablespoons cold water
4   eggs
½   pound ricotta
1   tablespoon warm water
     Salt
     Grated Parmesan cheese
     Olive oil

Blend flour and water, add eggs and beat 3 to 4 minutes. Mix ricotta with warm water, salt to taste and 1 tablespoon grated cheese.

Pour 1 tablespoon beaten egg in frying pan with a little heated oil. Cook until firm on bottom. Place 1 tablespoon ricotta mixture in center of omelet, overlapping edges toward center. Turn over carefully and brown. These small omelets may be served plain or with your favorite sauce.

ZUCCHINI OMELET

READY TRAY   Serves 4

3   zucchini, unpeeled, cut in thin rounds
2   tablespoons olive oil
4   eggs
½   teaspoon oregano
1   teaspoon chopped parsley
¼   teaspoon garlic powder, optional
     Salt and pepper

165

Sauté zucchini rounds in oil lightly.

Beat eggs with oregano, parsley, garlic powder, salt and pepper to taste. Pour over sautéed zucchini and cook slowly, browning both sides lightly, until omelet is firmly set. Cut in wedges to serve.

BASIC OMELET

READY TRAY   Serves 2

4 *eggs*
2 *tablespoons light cream*
   Salt and pepper
2 *tablespoons butter*

Whip eggs with cream, salt and pepper to taste, until light. Melt butter in frying pan over medium heat. Pour in eggs and when eggs become firm, roll edges toward center, and with spatula, turn over omelet gently and cook slowly 3 or 4 minutes.

Vegetables, grated cheese, diced meats or prosciutto may be added to the eggs before folding over.

SOUFFLÉ WITH PROSCIUTTO

READY TRAY

4 *eggs*
   Salt and pepper
2 *tablespoons grated Parmesan cheese*
¼ *pound thinly sliced prosciutto, cut in ½-inch strips*
½ *cup melted butter*

Separate eggs. Beat yolks light and whites until stiff.

Combine yolks, salt and pepper to taste, cheese and prosciutto. Fold in whites and butter carefully. Pour into greased soufflé dish or casserole. Bake uncovered in 350° oven, 20 minutes, until top is raised, lightly browned and puffed up. Serve immediately.

166

Desserts and Coffees

In Italy a meal is ended with fruit or cheese and not with pie, cake or ice cream as we do here, when we're not watching calories.

Making pastries, cakes, ices and ice creams is a job for the professional pastry cook—the *pasticciere*. The local pastry shop or caffe offers a selection of rich delicious pastries, all of which are too complicated and expensive for the housewife even to dream of making.

There are special cakes or pies or cookies made for each holiday, and the household can be thrown into a flurry of baking activity in preparation for the holiday. Since they're only made from time to time, thinking how good they're going to taste makes them doubly delicious.

The recipes given here are a mixture of simple and more complicated desserts.

FRUITS

Fruit is a very popular dessert on an Italian menu. Fresh fruit is served alone or with a selection of cheeses. Sometimes they are prepared ahead of time in a dry or sweet wine.

STRAWBERRIES WITH RED WINE

READY TRAY

1   basket strawberries, hulled, washed and drained
4   teaspoons sugar
1   cup red wine

Sprinkle sugar over berries, cover with wine and chill several hours before serving.

PEACHES WITH WINE

READY TRAY   Serves 4

4   fresh peaches
4   teaspoons sugar
½   cup wine, your choice

167

Peel and slice peaches. Sprinkle with sugar and pour wine over the slices. Mix lightly and refrigerate several hours before serving. Any fruit in season may be prepared in this delectable manner.

ICES

(GELATI)

READY TRAY

3 cups boiling water
3 cups sugar
  Juice ½ lemon
5 cups berries, your choice, pureed and seeds removed
  or
3 pounds fruit, your choice, peeled, pitted and pureed

Boil water and sugar until mixture drops from a spoon in threads. Cool thoroughly. Add lemon juice and fruit juice or pureed fruits. Mix thoroughly and freeze in ice-cream freezer or refrigerator trays for 30 to 40 minutes. Stir from time to time. The ice should not be frozen as hard as ice cream, but should be firm and smooth in texture. A small amount of liqueur may also be added for flavor.

Make this refreshing dessert when fresh fruits are at their peak. Serve in chilled goblets or parfait glasses.

RASPBERRY ICE

READY TRAY

1 cup sugar
2 cups water
2 cups raspberry puree or juice
  Juice ½ lemon
1 or 2 tablespoons raspberry liqueur
  Pitted black cherries

Combine sugar and water and bring to boil. Cook 5 minutes. Cool thoroughly. Add puree or juice, lemon juice and liqueur. Freeze in churn-type freezer or in refrigerator trays. If refrigerator trays are used, beat the ice when it reaches the mushy stage and every 30 minutes after that until it is ready to serve, to insure smoothness. Garnish with pitted black cherries.

CREAM FRITTERS

READY TRAY   Serves 4 to 6

4   egg yolks
¼   cup sugar
½   cup flour
     Salt to taste
4   cups milk, scalded
1   teaspoon grated orange or lemon rind
1   egg, beaten
     Breadcrumbs
2   tablespoons oil
2   tablespoons butter
     Powdered sugar
2   tablespoons brandy or rum

Beat egg yolks and sugar in top of double boiler. Cook over low heat, stirring with wooden spoon until slightly thickened. Mix in ¼ cup flour, salt and gradually add milk. Simmer, stirring, until very thick. At no time allow to boil. Blend in rind.

Rinse a square dish or pan with cold water and pour in mixture to a depth of 2 inches. Chill until firm. Cut into squares or rectangular pieces 2 inches long. Dip in remaining flour, in egg and then in breadcrumbs. Brown gently on both sides in hot oil and butter. Serve sprinkled with sugar, and flame with heated brandy or rum.

FRIED RICOTTA

READY TRAY   Serves 8

½   pound macaroons
1   pound ricotta cheese
     Pinch cinnamon
3   eggs
     Breadcrumbs
¼   pound butter
     Powdered sugar
     Brandy

169

Reduce macaroons to fine crumbs and blend until smooth with ricotta, cinnamon and 2 eggs. Roll into walnut-size balls. Dip them in beaten egg and roll in breadcrumbs. Brown in butter, sprinkle with sugar and brandy, and flame to serve.

RICOTTA PUDDING

READY TRAY   Serves 4 to 6

3   *tablespoons cream of wheat*
1   *pound ricotta cheese*
4   *tablespoons powdered sugar*
1   *whole egg*
1   *egg yolk (extra)*
1   *tablespoon candied fruit, chopped fine*
1   *tablespoon seedless raisins*
2   *tablespoons rum*
1   *egg white, beaten until stiff*
2   *tablespoons butter*
½   *cup breadcrumbs*

Cook cream of wheat in 1¼ cups water 5 minutes. Remove from heat and cool.

Blend thoroughly the ricotta, powdered sugar, whole egg, egg yolk, fruit, raisins, rum and cream of wheat. Fold in egg white carefully.

Butter a deep casserole and sprinkle bottom and sides with bread crumbs. Pour in mixture, bake uncovered in 375° oven for 1 hour.

ZABAGLIONE

(ITALIAN CUSTARD)

READY TRAY   Serves 4

5   *egg yolks*
5   *teaspoons sugar*
5   *half eggshells filled with wine: Marsala, tokay, sauterne, sherry or*
    other wine of your choice

A small round-bottomed copper-coated pan is made exclusively for this recipe. Lacking such a pan, the zabaglione can be prepared in the top of a double boiler.

Always use one more egg yolk than the number of servings desired.

Mix egg yolks, sugar and wine with a small wire whisk in top of double boiler until sugar is dissolved. Stir gently until mixture thickens from the sides toward the center, moving the cooked zabaglione to the center to allow the uncooked liquid to reach the sides of the pan. Do not stir too fast because this will curdle the eggs and spoil the zabaglione. The heat should be turned down so that the water is at a very slow and gentle simmer, never at a rolling boil.

If the water gets too hot, lift pan with custard out of the water for a few seconds but continue stirring. Then place over water again, until thickened. Pour into long-stemmed glasses.

Cognac may be used in place of wine. The dish is delicious laced with Chartreuse liqueur as it is poured into the serving glasses.

CANNOLI

READY TRAY   Makes 12

1½ cups flour
 1   tablespoon butter
     Pinch salt
 ½   teaspoon sugar
     Wine, sweet or dry

Mix flour, butter, salt and sugar. Add enough wine to make a stiff but workable dough. Form into ball and set aside 1 hour. Roll out dough ⅛ inch thick. Cut in 5-inch squares. Place cannoli tube (which may be purchased in specialty shops) across the corners of the square of dough. First fold one corner around the tube, then the other, and press together.

Fry in deep fat, one at a time, until dark golden brown. Remove the cannoli carefully and let cool before filling.

RICOTTA FILLING FOR CANNOLI

READY TRAY

1 *pound ricotta cheese*
2 *tablespoons rum*
2 *tablespoons sugar*
2 *tablespoons semisweet chocolate, chopped coarsely*
2 *tablespoons finely chopped candied fruit peel*

   Cream ricotta and rum until smooth. Add sugar, chocolate and candied fruit, and blend well.
   Fill cannoli tubes, sprinkle with powdered sugar and chill thoroughly before serving.

ANISE SLICES

READY TRAY   Makes about 2 dozen

2 *cups flour*
⅔ *cup sugar*
4 *tablespoons butter*
3 *eggs*
1 *tablespoon anise seeds*

   Separate eggs. Beat yolks light and whites until stiff. Combine egg yolks thoroughly with flour, sugar, butter and anise seeds. Fold in egg whites and mix until smooth.
   Butter and flour a loaf pan. Pour in batter and bake in 375° oven for 20 to 25 minutes. Remove from pan and cut in slices 1-inch thick. Place cut side down on buttered baking dish. Brown lightly on both sides for 10 minutes.

AMARETTI

(BITTERSWEET MACAROONS)

READY TRAY

⅓ *pound almonds, shelled*
2 *tablespoons bitter almonds*
1½ *cups powdered sugar*
3 *egg whites*

Blanch almonds and dry in warm oven for 5 to 10 minutes. Pound almonds to a fine powder in a mortar or electric blender. Combine with 1 egg white.

Beat remainder of egg whites stiff. Then add with powdered sugar to almonds, and blend until smooth.

Butter and flour a cookie sheet and drop dough by the teaspoonful 1 inch apart. Sprinkle with powdered sugar lightly, and set aside for 1 hour. Bake in 375° oven 5 to 10 minutes until lightly browned.

ITALIAN MACAROONS

READY TRAY

½ *pound almonds, shelled*
1 *cup sugar*
2 *egg whites, beaten until stiff*
½ *teaspoon almond extract*
  Butter
  Flour
  Powdered sugar

Blanch almonds and dry in 350° oven for 5 minutes. Pound as fine as possible in a mortar, or pass through a fine grinder. Blend with sugar, beaten egg whites and almond extract.

Butter a cookie sheet and dust with flour. Drop mixture by the teaspoonful 1 inch apart onto cookie sheet. Sprinkle with powdered sugar and set aside for 1 hour.

Bake in 375° oven until delicately browned, 5 to 7 minutes.

PANETTONE

(ITALIAN COFFEE CAKE)

READY TRAY

1 *package fresh or dried yeast*
1 *cup lukewarm water*
2 *pounds pastry flour*
6 *tablespoons butter*
6 *tablespoons sugar*
6 *egg yolks*
1 *teaspoon salt*
½ *cup seedless raisins*
½ *cup candied fruit, chopped*

173

Mix yeast with ½ cup lukewarm water, and set aside for 5 minutes.

Combine mixed yeast thoroughly with remaining water and enough flour to make a soft dough. Cover and set aside to rise in a warm place, for 1 hour. Add butter, sugar, egg yolks, salt, raisins, fruit and remaining flour. Knead on floured board until consistency of dough is elastic, about 15 minutes. Cover, set in warm place and let rise until double in bulk.

Shape into 1 large- or 2 medium-size round loaves. Place in greased baking pans, grease top of loaves, cover and let rise until double. Bake in 375° oven 1 hour until outside is well browned. Cool on wire racks away from drafts.

CAFFE ESPRESSO

READY TRAY   Makes 4 demitasses

4   tablespoons powdered Italian coffee
2   cups boiling water
Lemon peel or liqueur
Sugar to taste

Place coffee in middle strainer section of coffee machine (using home-style espresso machine). Pour water into water section and let steam through slowly, with cups underneath spout to catch steaming coffee.

Add twist of lemon peel to each cup, or a little liqueur if desired. Sugar to taste.

CAPPUCCINO

READY TRAY   Serves 2

1   heaping teaspoon ground chocolate
Hot water
½ cup milk, scalded
½ cup hot espresso coffee
or
1   teaspoon ground espresso coffee
1   jigger brandy, Cognac or rum
Sugar to taste
Cinnamon

174

Blend chocolate with enough hot water to make a thick paste in thick glass or chocolate mug. Blend with hot milk in top of double boiler and beat with wire whisk until frothy. Pour over hot coffee in glass or mug, add brandy and sugar and stir lightly. Garnish with a dash of cinnamon.

CAFFE PUNCHINO

READY TRAY

Coffee
½ *teaspoon sugar*
3 *whole cloves*
2 *lemon twists*
Brandy

This coffee is made directly in the cup at the table. Add sugar to a cup of coffee, break cloves into the coffee. Balance the bowl of a teaspoon on the lip of the coffee cup, float brandy, ignite, and while it is burning, twist the lemon peel through the fire. (Special spoons for this purpose may be obtained in some liquor stores.) This procedure creates a sparkling effect as the oil of the lemon rind comes in contact with the flame, to settle on the surface of the Punchino, with a slightly burned flavor.

FLAMING COFFEE DIABLE

READY TRAY   Serves 4

1 *bay leaf, torn in small pieces*
1 *cinnamon stick*
16 *coffee beans*
1 *tablespoon sugar*
1 *teaspoon whole cloves*
1 *orange, for rind and juice*
1 *grapefruit, for rind and juice*
1 *lemon, for rind and juice*
½ *cup Triple Sec liqueur*
½ *cup brandy*
⅓ *cup rum*
2 *cups strong, black, hot Italian coffee*

Make three chains of citrus rinds, 8 to 10 inches long. Puncture the chains at 2-inch intervals with whole cloves. In a deep pan heat the dry spices, sugar and coffee beans quickly over high heat.

Squeeze and strain the pulp of the orange, grapefruit and lemon into the heated spices and sugar. Hold the citrus chains together, gradually dribble the Triple Sec over them, set them aflame and allow to drip into the devil's brew. Fill pan with coffee, adding brandy and rum. Set aflame and strain with diable spoon. Serve in demitasse cups.

ABRUZZI, running from the Adriatic shore to central Italy, produces the light red *Montepulciano* and *Cerasuolo di Abruzzi* and the straw-colored *Trebbiano*, which does not travel well.

CAMPANIA. Wine is the finest in this province, of which Naples is the capital. Grown on the slopes of Mount Vesuvius, *Lacrima Christi* (the Tears of Christ) is the region's most famous wine. Other wines are *Falerno* and red *Gragnano*, which contain an essense of straw-berry in the bouquet.

EMILIA-ROMAGNA is one of the districts where vines grow among olives and wheat, and the wines are ordinary.

LOMBARDY. Here, the wines have to be created by hand because of the impossibility of using machinery on the steep mountains; only small quantities are obtainable. Among their red, white and rose wines the Pink is the finest.

PIEDMONT is the source of two of the best red wines, as well as vermouth and the sweet sparkling *Asti Spumante*. The famous reds are *Barolo and Barbaresco*. Barolo is a robust, rich red wine, which may fade with age to a light brownish color. It is excellent with all meat-sauce pastas.

SICILY is the home of the famous *Marsala*, blended from grape juice syrup and dried grapes and fermented with brandy. The white *Mamertina*, red *Faro* and the red and white wines of Etna are the finest of Sicilian table wines.

TRENTINO-ALTO ADIGE. The *Traminer* here is a white wine better than any other in Italy. The leading red wines are the plentiful *Teroldego*, dry and ruby red, and *Santa Maddalena*, which is smooth and clean.

TUSCANY. The red *Chianti* is at its best when young. One of the most recognized is *Brolio*, a classical Chianti produced by the firm of Ricasoli. Another beautiful product of Tuscany is the golden dessert *Vin Santo*.

VENETIA. Here, *Valpolicella* is the best and its bouquet is most delicate.

177

Glossary

Al burro   with butter
All'aglio   with garlic
All'aglio e olio   with garlic and oil
All'umido   cooked with just enough liquid to keep food moist
Al pesto   with crushed basil, garlic and olive oil
Amaretti   bittersweet macaroons
Apulian   as prepared in the province of Apulia
Au jus   served with the juices produced by the roast

Bagna cauda   a hot bath of oil and garlic in which vegetables are dipped
Basil   a popular aromatic herb
Bolognese   as prepared in Bologna
Broth   a concentrated stock

Cacciatore   Hunter style
Cannelloni   a variety of large filled pasta in the shape of pipes
Cannoli   an Italian pastry
Capers   the buds of a Mediterranean shrub
Cappelletti   ravioli made in the shape of a hat
Cardone   a vegetable, the leaves of which resemble those of the artichoke
Caul fat   a netlike thin sheet of fat which protects the inner organs of lamb and pork
Cioppino   a seafood stew popular in San Francisco
Diavolo (fra)   seasoned with hot peppers
Ditalini   a variety of macaroni in elbow-shaped pieces

Fagioli   beans
Fava   the oldest-known beans
Fennel   an aromatic vegetable
Fettuccine   a pasta cut in narrow strips
Filler   stuffing
Fretta (in)   in a hurry
Frittata   an Italian egg dish like an omelet

Genovese   as prepared in Genoa
Gnocchi   special Italian dumplings

Lasagne   broad noodles

Manicotti	a variety of filled pasta in the shape of muffs
Marinated	infused in herbs with wine, oil or vinegar
Marsala	a full bodied semisweet wine from Marsala, Sicily
Martinese	as prepared in Martina
Mezzani	a curved type of pasta
Milanese	as prepared in Milan
Minestra	a soup abundant in vegetables
Minestrone	a soup even more abundant in vegetables, with beans and pasta added
Mortadella	a variety of salami
Mostaccioli	a variety of macaroni cut diagonally
Neapolitan	as prepared in Naples
North Beach (alla)	as prepared in the North Beach section of San Francisco
Osso buco	veal shank
Panettone	Italian coffee cake
Pasta	all forms of macaroni and noodles
Pasta asciutta	pasta prepared with enough tomato sauce to cover each strand
Pastina	very small macaroni, usually used in soups
Peperoncini	little peppers, pickled
Pesto	condiment made of crushed basil, garlic and oil
Pimientos	a thick-fleshed pepper (usually red)
Piquant	pungent or tart taste
Pizza	a bread-dough pie seasoned with oil, tomato, cheese, etc.
Polenta	mush made with coarse cornmeal
Prosciutto	Italian-cured ham
Provolone	an Italian variety of cheese
Pugliese	as prepared in the province of Puglia
Radichetti	a bitter vegetable
Ramekin	a casserole-type dish used for both baking and serving
Ravioli	a pasta dough filled with a stuffing and cut in squares
Ricotta	an Italian cheese similar to cottage cheese, made mainly from milk whey of cow, sheep or goat
Rigatoni	a form of short hollow pasta, curved and fluted
Risotto	rice cooked in a special Italian way
Rollatine	small meat rolls, stuffed
Rollatone	large meat roll, stuffed
Romano	a variety of Italian cheese; also, as prepared in Rome
Sautéed	cooked quickly over a high flame in a little oil or shortening to extract the water contained in the meat
Scaloppine	thin slices of veal

179

Tagliarini	a narrow ribbon-like form of pasta; noodles
Tarantino	as prepared in Taranto
Tarragon	a leaf known for its aromatic quality
Tenderpods	pods of beans or beans tender enough to be cooked without shelling them
Tortellini	a form of ravioli in the shape of half-moons
Truffles	underground fungi resembling the mushroom; the Alba ones are the most flavorful

Zabaglione	an Italian custard made with wine, sugar and eggs
Ziti	a large variety of macaroni
Zucchini	small squashes

Index

Index

A

185

F

G

I

K

L

190

W

Z